Camera Angles

Tips and Techniques for Professional-Quality Photographs

Camera Angles

Tips and Techniques for Professional- Quality Photographs

By Rick Sammon
America's Most Popular Photo Expert!

VOYAGEUR PRESS

Edited by Kathryn Mallien • Cover designed by Zachary J. Marell
Printed in Canada
94   95   96   97   98   5   4   3   2   1

Library of Congress Cataloging-in-Publication Data
Sammon, Rick.
     Camera angles : tips and techniques for professional-quality photographs
        (by America's most popular photo expert) / by Rick Sammon.
     p.   cm.
     Includes index.
     ISBN 0-89658-235-3
     1. Photography.   I. Title.
     TR145.S23   1994
     771—dc20   93–21364
                     CIP

Published by VOYAGEUR PRESS, INC.
P.O. Box 338, 123 North Second Street, Stillwater, MN 55082 U.S.A.
612-430-2210

Please write or call, or stop by, for our free catalog of natural history, travel, and photography publications. Our TOLL-FREE number to place an order or to obtain a free catalog is 800-888-WOLF (800-888-9653).

Educators, fundraisers, premium and gift buyers, publicists, and marketing managers: Looking for creative products and new sales ideas? Voyageur Press books are available at special discounts when purchased in quantities, and special editions can be created to your specifications. For details contact the marketing department.

Distributed in Canada by RAINCOAST BOOKS
112 East Third Avenue, Vancouver, BC V5T 1C8

Dedication

For the great Grand Canyon photographer
Charlie "C.B." Bray—thank you.

Contents

Foreword

Composing for color in a photograph is just as important as composing for a subject. (photo #1, page 49)

It seems that every time I see Rick Sammon, he's wearing a khaki bush shirt with epaulets and flapped pockets, as though he has just returned from some adventure or is about to embark on one. I take this as a legitimate hallmark because Rick truly is a well-traveled, do-it-all photographer, and as such has a great deal to share with the readers of this book.

If experience is the greatest teacher, then Rick's resume already represents a lifetime's worth. When I first met him, he was working as a vice president at a public relations firm, a job that gave him insight into the hardware side of the business. At the same time and still today, he manages CEDAM International, an exploration organization dedicated to Conservation, Education, Diving, Archeology, and Museums; he's also a member of the Explorers Club. This is the "Establishment" Rick.

Rick is uncommonly prolific. He is a regular contributor to *Outdoor Photographer* and acts as our East Coast correspondent. His Associated Press column, with approximately 2.5 million readers each week, has the distinction of being the most widely read photo column in the United States . . . maybe even the world. Other writing credits in various periodicals are too numerous for me to recount. Now in 1994, Rick will publish five books on photography and nature subjects: two with the Nature Company and three with Voyageur Press.

What's most important is that Rick can *do* it as well as *teach*. Working on photographic projects that range from *Sports Illustrated* swim-suit models to Baikal seals in Siberia, he has "been there, done that" for a variety of locations and assignments equaled by few other photographers that I know. Under the banner of CEDAM, he organized an enormous marine conservation project on the "Seven Underwater Wonders of the World," which spawned a book, a series of posters, two calendars, and an upcoming television documentary.

One final credit makes all of the above even more impressive: Rick does it all while being a husband and father. Among globe-trotting photographers, that makes him a member of a very select group.

Steve Werner
Editor and Publisher,
Outdoor Photographer *magazine*
1994

Introduction: Why I Take Pictures

For me, a good photo-graph is one that cap-tures a precious mo-ment in time.
(photo #2, page 50)

I take many different types of pictures. Most of my top-side pictures are self-assignments for "Camera Angles" and the other columns I write for photography magazines. These pictures illustrate a specific photographic technique. It's my hope that each photo column helps newcomers to the world of photography get more joy out of taking pictures.

I also take lots of pictures under water. When shooting in this environment, I try to take pictures that convey the beauty and wonder of the marine environment to non-divers. These photographs also serve as a permanent record of the fragile coral reef ecosystem for future generations. They show the state of the different ecosystems as they are today. Hopefully, these pictures will not be the only way for future generations to see the beauty of the underwater environment. Here, again, I use photography as a teaching tool.

When photographing in a far-off land, above or under water, I get a tremendous sense of satisfaction from holding a camera and looking through the viewfinder at new sites and people. In composing a scene, I capture a part of the world as I see it, for my own enjoyment.

For me, this enjoyment is what photography is all about, whether I'm photographing a seal in Lake Baikal, Siberia, or my son in my kitchen. Both of these pictures capture a frozen moment in time—a moment that I can relive whenever I page through my photo album or review my slides.

I hope this collection of my favorite AP photo columns gives you a good understanding of what it takes to get good pictures in many different shooting situations. As you'll see, the text is geared toward 35mm SLR "shooters." The beginner will find lots of important basic information here, and the advanced amateur will learn special techniques to add to his or her photography repetoire. After you read about a particular subject, I suggest that you take lots of pictures. Don't be discouraged by your mistakes. Keep on shooting. This is how you will learn what makes a good picture.

Someday, your photographs will be an important record of what you have seen, who you have met, and where you have traveled. They will bring back great memories, and give your children and your children's children a unique view of our world as seen by a very special individual . . . you!

If you plan to sell your photographs, my advice is to keep your slides in circulation. They do you absolutely no good resting in your files.

Good Luck.

Rick Sammon
Croton-on-Hudson, New York
1994

Part 1:
Getting Started

Good Technique

One of the first steps on the long road to becoming a good photographer is to familiarize yourself with the technical aspects of picture-taking. You need to learn about how shutter speeds blur or freeze action, how *f*-stops affect depth of field, how different lenses change the perspective of a scene, and how films and filters change the mood of a photograph.

Although mastering the technical aspects of picture-taking will make for good technique, it does not necessarily make for a good photographer. So, if good technique is not the key element in picture-taking, what's needed to turn snapshots into great shots?

To find the answer to this question, I talked to some of the top professional photographers in the country.

Al Moldvay, a former *National Geographic* photographer, feels that photographs should have a message. "To me, the primary function of photography is to tell a story," Al explained. "I think of a photograph this way: What do I want to say? What is the best way to say it? How can I make it as artistic as possible? Although I don't consider myself to be an art photographer, I always try to put an artistic twist on my pictures. I agree that too many amateur photographers get caught up in the technique, especially in the technique of using lenses. It's not the lens that makes the statement, it's only the means to the statement."

Fashion photographer Rebecca Blake agrees that a good photograph goes beyond technique.

Good photographs are a result of your interests, good technique, and the special way you see a subject. (photo #4, page 51)

"In order to be a good photographer, one should nourish his or her interest in photography and bring other things into it," she said. "My own nourishment comes from trying to be aware of everything that is happening around me."

Robert Farber, known for his art-quality images, feels inspiration is important, too. "When I was younger, I used to spend my weekends at art galleries and museums. I studied the work of the impressionistic painters to see how they dealt with light and shadows," he said. "The softness and beauty of these paintings prompted me to experiment with different films and filters. I wanted to see how grain and softness affected my pictures. I tried to duplicate in my photographs the feeling I got when I looked at these paintings."

Arthur Rothstein has one of the most important tips for amateur photographers. "In order to make a good photograph, you must learn how to 'see' light," he said. "Many beginner photographers take people pictures that have no light in the eyes. They don't realize that the eyes are perhaps the most important part of the picture; they are the mirror of the soul."

Good photographs are truly the result of the way you see a subject. Consider your own interests when selecting a subject. If you like wildlife and the great outdoors, you'll probably have a good feel for nature photography. If you enjoy music, the local jazz club or pub may provide some good photo opportunities. And if you love children, you might even get some award-winning portraits right in your own living room.

Five Ingredients for a Good Photo

An amateur photographer once asked me a good question: "What do I need to take great pictures?"

I thought about that for a while, and came up with five basic elements that I think are essential for taking outstanding pictures—pictures that capture the viewer's imagination, that are more than mere snapshots, and that have a professional look.

Subject. An interesting subject is the first thing you'll need to make a great photograph. Of course, you could travel to the Grand Canyon, Hong Kong, Paris, or New York City to find interesting subjects. But you don't have to travel that far to get great pictures. Investigate your neighborhood park, where you might spot two children playing in a field, or a duck backlit on a pond. Or spend a day at the zoo, where you'll find dozens of interesting subjects in their natural surroundings.

No matter where you shoot, the key to good pictures is learning how to selectively isolate your subject from distracting elements in the scene. Note the background and foreground, and determine whether or not they will enhance your picture. Careful composition and unique angles can even make an ordinary subject look interesting.

The elements needed to make a good picture include an interesting subject, dependable camera equipment, film that can record the true color of your subject, practice, and last but not least, luck.
(photo #3, page 50)

Camera. A dependable camera with sharp optics is a must for the serious photographer. For the ultimate in flexibility and creativity, you'll want to shoot with a 35mm SLR (single-lens reflex) camera.

There are several reasons for choosing an SLR. You view the scene through the lens, so as far as composition goes, what you see is what you get. Accessory lenses are available for SLRs for macro, wide-angle, standard, telephoto, and super telephoto photography. And optional flash units give you the opportunity to experiment with both on- and off-camera lighting.

Film. There are dozens of films available, and each photographer has his or her favorite. However, it's important to keep in mind what you want to accomplish with your picture, because there are films better suited for certain situations.

Kodak publishes a guide to help you determine which films will meet your shooting requirements. This film guide is available at your local photography dealer. If you are new to photography, I strongly recommend that you read it. For now, the chapter Films and Filters offers practical information.

Practice. "Practice make perfect" is a cliché, but it's true nonetheless. Hours of practice around your house will pay off later—when you may not have time to practice. If you spend some time at home becoming familiar with your camera's capabilities, you'll be able to concentrate in the field on getting great pictures, without wasting time figuring out your camera's knobs and dials.

Luck. Although some professional photograhers may not want to admit it, luck is essential for getting eye-catching images. There are two ways to improve your luck. First, get out and shoot as often as possible. The more you see, the better chance you'll have of getting a great picture. Second, work hard at your photography. The harder you work, the luckier you'll be.

SLRs vs. Point-and-Shoot Cameras

When shooting with an SLR camera, you can add accessories that expand your photographic horizons, such as a wide-angle lens for good depth of field and a polarizing filter to darken the sky. (photo #6, page 52)

Here's a typical conversation heard in a camera store:

Customer: I'm interested in buying a 35mm autofocus camera. I've never taken pictures before, so I need a camera that's simple to operate. And I want good results. What do you recommend for about $300?

Salesperson: Are you looking for an SLR or a fixed-lens camera?

Customer: What's the difference?

Salesperson: SLR stands for single-lens-reflex. With an SLR camera, you can choose from many different focal length lenses for a variety of different perspectives. The fixed-lens camera, on the other hand, has only one lens, but it's usually a zoom that actually functions as many lenses in one.

Customer: It sounds like both cameras do the same thing and take the same kind of pictures. Are there any other differences?

Salesperson: Well, some fixed-lens cameras have infrared, five-beam autofocusing, a 3x zoom range, and DX coding, which automatically sets film speed. Most SLRs have similar features, but also offer matrix metering, shutter speeds up to 1/8000 second, and even a metering range of EV 1 to EV 21 at ISO 100 with a $f/1.4$ lens.

Customer (looking confused and nervous): Uh, excuse me. I'm sorry, but I've gotta run. I'll come back. Thanks for the information.

The moral of this little encounter is this: Choosing a camera can be pretty tough, and even a bit scary. But a little knowledge about the features and benefits of both camera types can go a long way for the first-time buyer and may save you from making the costly mistake of purchasing a camera not suited for your needs.

SLR. Single-lens-reflex cameras are so called because you view the scene exactly as the camera sees it: through the lens that is on the front of the camera. The benefit is that you get on film the exact composition that you see in the viewfinder. There are no surprises in your pictures, such as "cut-off" feet or distracting signs or branches in the corner of the frame. With a fixed-lens camera, on the other hand, you don't get exactly what you see, because you view the scene through a framefinder, not through the lens. For the majority of picture-taking situations, this really does not make a difference. But if you are a purist, you'll want an SLR.

The main advantage of taking pictures with an SLR is the choice of lenses that lets you capture everything from a sweeping landscape (wide-angle lenses) to close-ups of sports action from the sidelines (telephoto lenses). Accessories such as data backs, remote control units, and sophisticated on- and off-camera flash units make the SLR system attractive to those who want to expand their photographic horizons.

Finally, most SLRs offer both automatic and manual exposure, so you can be creative with lighting, depth of field, and freezing or blurring subject movement. SLRs are a must for professional photographers and are desirable for advanced amateur picture-takers. For high school students who really want to learn about photography, a 35mm automatic SLR camera with manual exposure override would make a great gift.

Fixed-lens cameras. Fixed-lens cameras, also known as lens-shutter cameras or point-and-shoot cameras, traditionally are fully automatic. Your creative options lie mainly in composition (although newer models let you control the flash to a degree).

Most of today's fixed-lens cameras feature built-in zoom lenses for medium-wide-angle and medium-telephoto shots. Smaller and lighter than SLRs, these cameras deliver very good pictures. However, enlargements bigger than eleven by fourteen inches may not be as sharp and crisp as those taken with SLRs because the camera's optics often are not as sophisticated.

If you want to travel extremely light and simply want to compose and shoot, you'll enjoy using a fixed-lens camera.

If you are seriously considering buying a camera for yourself or as a gift, it's a good idea to do a little homework before you shop. *Outdoor Photographer*, a monthly magazine available on newsstands, features columns on the latest and greatest in new cameras, as well as tips and tricks for great photos. It can save you from a lengthy Q & A session at your photo dealer.

In addition, free brochures published by major manufacturers are available at your local dealer. If you go on a scouting mission and do some research, you'll be fairly sure of which camera is best for you.

Choosing the Right Lens

While reading a photography magazine, I noticed the following tag line in an ad: "More than 50 lenses are available for our 35mm SLR camera." I thought, Wow! What a wonderful thing for a professional photographer who needs to shoot in a variety of situations. But then I thought, What about the amateur or beginner in photography who doesn't know the differences between lenses?

To help you determine which lens or lens system is just right for you, here's a quick look at what's available. (Please note that focal lengths may vary from one camera/lens manufacturer to another.)

Normal or standard lenses. A 35mm AF (autofocus) SLR camera usually is sold with a 50mm lens, known as a normal or standard lens. It's so called because it has an angle of view similar to our normal field of vision. This is a good, inexpensive starter lens if you're new to the world of 35mm photography.

Wide-angle lenses. If you want to capture sweeping landscapes with good depth of field, you'll need a wide-angle lens. Wide-angle lenses range in focal length from 20mm to 35mm, with the smaller-number lenses having the wider view. **Ultra-wide-angle lenses** (14mm to 18mm) capture even more of the scene than wide-angle lenses, and they offer tremendous depth of field.

Different lenses are designed for different shooting situations. For this photo, I used a 24mm wide-angle lens for foreground-to-infinity sharpness. (photo #5, page 52)

Although wide-angle lenses are great for capturing sweeping panoramas, they also can be used for dramatic close-up photographs with great depth of field.

To capture the widest possible view with one lens, there are fish-eye lenses (6mm to 8mm) that provide an angle of view of 180 degrees and produce a circular image on the rectangular 35mm frame.

Telephoto lenses. If you want to take portraits of faraway people or animals, you'll need a telephoto lens. Like wide-angle lenses, telephoto lenses are available in a variety of focal lengths, from 85mm to 1600mm. The longer the lens, the more powerful the magnification. Longer focal length lenses, like wider ones, feature more glass and complex optics. Therefore, they are quite expensive.

Zoom lenses. Ah, my favorite category. Zooms are perhaps the most popular lenses. Their advantage is that they provide several focal lengths (or several lenses) in one lens. My favorite zoom for wildlife photography is a 180–600mm lens. It's a bit heavy, but it gives me medium- and super-telephoto views—and everything in between. There are other zooms available from AF SLR camera manufacturers, including 100–300mm, 28–85mm, and 35–200mm zooms. Remember, the greater the zoom range, the more versatile (and expensive) the lens.

Macros, mirrors, and teleconverters. If you like to shoot close-ups of flowers and insects, you'll need a macro lens. This lens produces high magnification and lets you get close to your subject.

If you don't want to invest in a macro lens, which can cost anywhere from $250 to $600, you may want to try a set (usually three) of close-up lenses, which sell for under $50. These lenses, each of which offers a different magnification, can be screwed into the filter thread on the front of lenses with focal lengths from 35mm to 55mm. For maximum magnification, the three close-up lenses can be used together. Naturally, screw-in close-up lenses don't produce the razor sharp images that macro lenses produce.

Mirror lenses use mirrors to cut down on the length of super telephoto lenses. For example, a 500mm mirror lens may be only 150mm long—a nice feature if you need to travel light.

Teleconverters double the effective focal length of a lens. For example, a teleconverter on a 100mm lens gives the lens an effective focal length of 200mm. The main advantage is that you can pack a relatively small teleconverter in your camera bag and double your lens's focal length at will.

AF vs. non-AF lenses. Today, just about every 35mm SLR camera manufacturer offers autofocus cameras and lenses, most of which focus faster than we humans can.

I'm often asked if autofocus lenses are better than non-autofocus lenses. My reply is simple: "Do you ever want to take an out-of-focus picture of an animal or nature scene?"

On most basic AF cameras, the autofocus sensor (or sensors—more sophisticated models have more sensors) is in the center of the frame and the AF viewfinder mark is in the center of the viewfinder. This means that whatever is in the center of the frame will be in sharp focus.

For AF pictures of off-center subjects, most AF SLRs (and most lens-shutter cameras) have what is called a focus lock, which is activated by pressing the shutter release button ever so slightly. Once you focus on the main subject and lock in the focus, you simply recompose and shoot for a sharp picture.

One drawback to some AF telephoto and telephoto zoom lenses is that they are difficult to focus in low-light situations. Some new models have remedied this by including on-camera or on-flash AF illuminators, which project an infrared pattern on the subject to allow autofocusing. However, if the subject is out of the range of the infrared beam, you still may have to focus manually.

Here's one final tip on using lenses: To avoid blurred pictures caused by camera shake, never shoot at a shutter speed lower than the focal length of the lens. Two examples: If you are shooting with a 50mm lens, select a shutter speed faster than 1/60 second; if you're shooting with a 500mm lens, don't choose a shutter speed slower than 1/500 second.

Zoom Lenses

Take a look at this photo of Jimmy Carter (page 55). Now, cover Mr. Carter's hand. See how the impact of the photograph has been diminished? If I had not had a 80–200mm zoom lens while covering the meeting at which President Carter was speaking, I would have missed the message and strength of the moment.

You see, my 300mm telephoto lens would have produced a closely cropped head-and-shoulders shot—static and without impact. My trusty zoom lens, on the other hand, let me creatively compose my photograph in the camera, so although I was locked into a very limiting shooting position, I was not locked into a limited view of my subject. This is one reason why zoom lenses are so popular: flexibility.

Years ago, zoom lenses were not as sharp as fixed focal length lenses. In fact, many professional photographers would not have been caught dead with a zoom lens. Most of today's zooms, however, are highly sophisticated accessories that deliver superb results, for professional and amateur photographers alike. This is due to improvements in lens design (mostly accomplished with the aid of computers) and improved lens coatings, which help reduce flare and internal lens reflections.

Leading camera manufacturers offer many zoom lenses for their 35mm autofocus SLR cameras. Some of the more popular zoom ranges are 24–50mm, good for landscape and standard photography; 35–70mm, well suited for people pictures and photojournalism; and 80–200mm,

Zoom lenses give you flexibility over composition without changing your position. This is big advantage when you are locked into a shooting location. (photo #11, page 55)

25

designed for portrait and wildlife photography.

The main advantage to using a zoom lens is that you can travel relatively light, with perhaps only a lens or two in your camera bag. The one drawback to most zooms is that they have a relatively small maximum aperture, or lens opening, so less light reaches the film. These small apertures (*f*/4 or *f*/5.6) dictate the use of slower shutter speeds. However, with all the outstanding fast films available today, this really is not a problem. If you shoot with a film with a rating of ISO 200 or higher, you shouldn't have a problem using a zoom in daylight conditions. If you do get into a situation where the shutter speed is so slow that you can't hand-hold your camera, simply use a tripod or monopod, brace yourself securely against a nearby object, or switch to a higher speed film.

There are fast zoom lenses available with maximum apertures of *f*/2.8 that do indeed let you shoot in low light situations. The disadvantage is that they are more expensive than slower zooms having the same focal length.

Films and Filters

Films. Once you've chosen a camera and lenses, the next important decision to make is what type of films to use. This is no easy task, considering that the leader in the film business, Kodak, offers more than a dozen consumer films and a dozen professional films for 35mm cameras.

Professional films are for professional photographers and consumer films are for amateurs, right? Well, not necessarily. Professional films are manufactured to a specific color standard and are then refrigerated by the manufacturer and retailer. This process maintains the color standard until the film is ready for use. Pros use these films because color is often extremely critical in portrait and commercial photography; they know they can count on pro films to deliver consistent color. They, too, keep the film in the refrigerator until ready for use.

If you want to try some of the professional films, you can find them at a professionals' camera store or color lab. These films are clearly marked as professional films, and are slightly more expensive than consumer films.

Consumers usually are less particular about color, and most don't store film in a refrigerator. Therefore, consumer films are manufactured to "mature" to a specific color standard about nine months after purchase (the average time it takes for consumer films to get into consumers' cameras). Consumer films also can be refrigerated, and will deliver excellent color even years after the expiration date.

You also need to choose between slide and

A polarizing filter can reduce glare on water and brighten white clouds against a blue sky. Fine-grain film produces ultra-sharp pictures.
(photo #7, page 53)

print film. Although you can make slides from print films and vice versa, doing this can be expensive. Therefore, it's best to shoot with a film that meets your exact needs.

Most professional photographers shoot slide film, while most amateurs shoot prints. Slide film processing is less expensive than print film processing, so if you plan to shoot lots and lots of pictures, slide film is more economical. And, because book and magazine publishers usually require that photo submissions be in slide form, you should shoot slides if you have hopes of publishing your work.

One disadvantage of slide film is that your exposure must be perfect, or you'll end up with an image that's too dark or too light. Print film, on the other hand, has what's called a wide exposure latitude; if you have not set your camera correctly, you'll still get a very good print.

The next thing to consider is film speed. All films have what's called an ISO number (also called exposure index), indicating the film's relative sensitivity to light. "Fast" films have high ISO numbers and require less light for proper exposure than "slow" films. Therefore, in a setting with little light, you'll need to shoot with a fast film (ISO 400 or 1000). As the light level increases, the required ISO number decreases. When shooting during bright daylight hours, you'll use slow to medium films (ISO 50 to 100).

Slow films (ISO 25 and 50) have extremely fine grain, and are superb if you want to make large prints from your slides or negatives. However, they usually require slow shutter speeds. This is fine for landscape photography, but is not recommended for action shooting.

For sports and action photography, fast films (ISO 400, 1000, and even 1600) produce the best results. These films allow you to shoot at high shutter speeds that "freeze" the action in a scene, and are very light sensitive, so you can shoot without a flash in churches, museums, and concert halls. Fast films also have larger grain, which can be distracting and may make an image look soft. This isn't always a disadvantage; the soft effect caused by large grain can enhance early morning and late afternoon landscapes, seascapes, and wildlife photos.

Between slow and fast films there are "medium speed" films (ISO 64, 100, 125, and 200). These films are ideal for general picture taking, and are a good choice when you want to keep your camera loaded and ready for shooting.

New films are constantly being introduced. Kodak recently unveiled two consumer color print films: Kodak Gold Plus 100 and Gold Plus 200. These new films offer extended performance under a wider range of picture-taking situations than did the earlier Kodak Gold 100 and 200. Now, even if your exposure is slightly over or under the correct exposure, you will still get an excellent image.

To determine what film is best for your particular needs, buy a few rolls of different kinds, do some test shooting, and compare the results. A backyard test may prevent a frustration attack when you are shooting away from home.

Filters. Like the right film, the right filter can help you expand your photographic horizons and enable you to capture events in less than ideal situations. Filters are attached directly over the lens of your camera. When using filters on an automatic exposure camera, you don't have to make any exposure adjustments because the light is still coming through the lens and is being measured by the camera's metering system. This holds true even if two or more filters are used simultaneously.

Two handy filters will enhance many of your outdoor photographs. A polarizing filter can reduce glare on water and darken white clouds against a blue sky. It also can reduce glare on leaves in landscape pictures, allowing for richer colors in the end-result photo. Many pros use a polarizing filter for all their outdoor pictures.

Another useful filter is a skylight or haze filter. This filter reduces the bluish cast ultraviolet light gives outdoor photographs—especially beach and snow scenes. It also helps to reduce the softening effect of atmospheric haze, giving your outdoor pictures a crisper look.

There are a variety of other filters available. In fact, creative filter systems offer professional and amateur photographers more than one hundred filters that can be used to improve your photos and create special effects. You might experiment with a fog filter, which gives sunlit scenes a misty appearance; or a half-blue, half-clear graduated filter, which turns a gray sky into a blue sky. A sunset filter transforms a midday setting into a sunset scene, and a star filter converts intense points of light to stars.

To see what filters can add to your photography, stop by your local photo dealer. He or she will most likely have a filter chart with before and after pictures illustrating the advantages of shooting with each type of filter.

Don't overlook the importance of these relatively small and inexpensive accessories. They can make all the difference.

Getting the Right Exposure

Photography is the science, art, and craft of exposing film to light. Getting good exposure is what photography is all about. However, because different photographers like to create different moods with their pictures, by emphasizing shadows or highlights, a "good" exposure means different things to different people. In addition, the "correct" exposure according to an in-camera light meter is not always the best exposure. Here are three examples.

Underexposure. By slightly underexposing a scene, you increase the color saturation of your subject; thus, you get richer colors but a slightly darker picture. Many pros, as well as fine art book and magazine art directors, prefer these richer colors. To get the right effect, underexpose your pictures by one-quarter stop using the ISO dial. For example, expose ISO 50 film at 64, ISO 64 film at 80, and so on.

Another way to intentionally underexpose a frame is to use the +/- exposure compensation feature found on most top-of-the-line 35mm AF SLRs.

Correct exposure. At the "correct" exposure, your *overall* scene may have a pleasing exposure, but your shadow areas may be too dark and your highlight areas may be washed out. In situations where you have a variety of light levels, you have several options for getting a good

In-camera light meters make it relatively easy to get a good exposure when a scene is evenly lit. In tricky backlit lighting situations, however, bracketing is essential for a correct exposure.
(photo #8, page 54)

exposure of the main subject or main area of interest. With an automatic/manual exposure camera, take a light reading of the main subject (by filling the frame with the subject) in the auto mode and then manually set your exposure to that reading. Or, if your camera has a built-in spot meter or automatic exposure lock, meter the main subject, lock in the reading, recompose the scene, and then make your exposure.

Another option is to use a gray card (available at camera stores). Take a reading of the light falling on the card and manually set your camera to that reading. Or, if the scene you're shooting has too much contrast, you may have to add light with an on-camera flash to compress the brightness ratio.

When photographing scenes with lots of contrast, such as a landscape with a bright sky and deep shadows on mountains, it's important to remember one of the golden rules of photography: When shooting slide film, expose for the *brightest* area in a scene; with print film, expose for the *shadow* areas.

Overexposure. Technically overexposing a subject or scene often results in a washed out picture. This is not the case if you're photographing a beach or snow in bright sunlight—two situations that can fool a camera's light meter into thinking that the scene is brighter than it actually is. If you shoot on automatic in these situations, you'll probably get an underexposed picture. But by slightly overexposing your picture (by one stop), you'll get the correctly exposed image on film. For guaranteed good results, bracket your exposures.

You also need to slightly overexpose a frame

when you are photographing someone with very dark skin tones. Again, more light on a dark subject is needed for correct exposure.

When evaluating a scene for exposure, it's important to note that your eyes are *much* more sensitive to light than are standard color and black and white films. Therefore, the shadows and highlights you see in a scene may not be exactly what's recorded on film. So, to get a "correct" exposure, bracket! Some pros bracket in quarter stops in each direction, to +1 over the recommended setting and then to -1 under the recommended setting, to get the best exposure. That's seven exposures just to get one great picture, but it's worth the resulting four great shots per roll of film!

Exposure Modes

Automatic exposure
modes usually produce
picture-perfect results.
For this photo, the Pro-
gram mode automati-
cally selected and set
the aperture and shut-
ter speed for correct
exposure.
(photo #10, page 55)

It doesn't matter what kind of 35mm AF SLR camera you have. You can, with some basic photography knowledge, get great flash and natural light pictures by shooting in the automatic exposure mode.

The 35mm AF SLR camera manufacturers employ highly skilled camera engineers who design state-of-the-art automatic exposure systems. In most cases, these systems are guided by micro computers and sophisticated light reading sensors, which set the f-stop and/or shutter speed in a split second. The result of this technology and research is that you can get a high percentage of good pictures without having to fuss with knobs, dials, or tricky exposure calculations.

Of course, there are certain situations, especially when photographing high-contrast scenes, when manual exposure is required. In addition, manual metering and manual exposure settings may be preferred over shooting on automatic when you want to fine-tune a slide exposure. However, making exposure readings takes time, as does setting the f-stop and shutter speed. In some cases, by the time you've finished making all the necessary settings, you may have missed that once-in-a-lifetime picture. So, shooting on automatic may oftentimes be preferred to shooting in the manual mode.

Different 35mm AF SLR camera manufacturers offer different automatic exposure modes in their cameras. Some low-end models feature only one type of AE system, usually Program or

Aperture Priority. At the other end of the spectrum (and price range) are AE cameras that feature several different types of systems. Before you buy a camera, it's important to consider which AE system or systems will suit your needs.

Aperture Priority (A). You select the aperture (lens opening) and the camera automatically selects the appropriate shutter speed (length of time that the shutter remains open) for the correct exposure. This mode is useful when depth of field is important, such as in landscape and flash macro photography.

Shutter Priority (S). You select the shutter speed and the camera automatically selects the correct aperture. This is the appropriate mode to use when stopping action in natural light photos, particularly in sports events.

Program (P). The camera selects both the shutter speed and f-stop for correct exposure. This mode takes all the guesswork out of determining exposure. It's useful in situations when you simply don't have time to make camera adjustments, or when you would rather concentrate fully on creative composition.

Some AF SLR cameras, such as the Canon EOS-1, feature a standard Program mode plus two additional program modes: Program D (depth) mode, which selects an exposure setting with a smaller f-stop for more depth of field than you'd get in the standard Program mode; and Program H (high speed) mode, which selects a higher shutter speed than would be set in the standard Program mode. The EOS also features Aperture Priority and Shutter Priority automation, plus manual exposure control.

35

When shooting in any AE mode, you'll get the best results if you fill the frame with the subject. This technique usually provides the camera's light meter with an evenly illuminated area, thus providing an even exposure.

Another way to get the most out of an AE system is to shoot print film, which has a wider exposure latitude than slide film has. A wide exposure latitude means that your exposure can be a stop or two over the "correct" exposure and you'll still get a good-looking print.

When to Focus Manually

When choosing an autofocus camera, one key feature to look for is manual focusing. Autofocus systems can be "fooled" in several picture-taking situations, and it's important to be able to override the camera's automatic mechanism.

For example, in low-light/low contrast situations, some early model AF SLRs can't focus quickly or accurately. With these cameras, it actually may be faster to focus manually. However, some of the newer AF SLRs feature built-in AF illuminators (which project infrared light patterns on subjects) and sophisticated light metering systems (which require only the light from one candle). These cameras deliver sharp pictures even in near darkness—or in the dark for that matter.

Some early model AF SLRs also have difficulty finding focus because the lenses have a tendency to cycle back and forth throughout the entire focus range of the lens. This is particularly true for telephoto lenses (most normal-to-wide-angle lenses focus quickly). As a solution, some newer AF SLR telephoto lenses are fitted with a "limit" button which, when activated, limits the range of focus search. In addition, newer AF SLRs have a higher speed AF motor in the camera body (or even in the lens itself) that increases the focus search speed, and much more sensitive AF sensors.

Because most AF SLRs have AF sensors in

Sophisticated 35mm AF SLR cameras provide fast focus in the majority of shooting situations. But in low-light situations, it may actually be faster to focus manually. (photo #9, page 55)

the center of the frame, getting sharp pictures of off-center subjects takes additional time. It is usually a toss-up whether to center the subject in the frame, use the AF lock button, recompose the photo and shoot, or to opt for manual focusing.

Some newer model 35mm autofocus SLRs feature more AF sensors in the frame than older models. Others have a wider AF sensor area. In most cases, the AF system defaults to the closest subject in the viewfinder.

Some models use four sensors (two for subjects with horizontal lines and two for subjects with vertical lines). With this type of AF system, you also can select individual sensors. In addition, the sensitivity area of the sensors automatically changes when you hold the camera in the vertical position.

Manual focus is useful if you want to focus on an area and wait for a subject to enter the frame, such as the finish line at a horse race or a runner reaching home plate.

It also may be preferable to switch to manual focus when using teleconverters in conjunction with telephoto lenses. Because teleconverters cut the light passing through the lens by one or two stops, it may make autofocusing unuseable, sporadic, or just too slow.

It's important to remember that autofocus is like autoexposure in one respect: You can shoot on automatic or manual—it's your choice.

Part 2:
Advanced
Techniques

Creative Composition

One of the most common mistakes amateur photographers make, especially those using autofocus cameras, is always placing the subject in the center of the frame. This can result in a good photograph; however, a photograph in which the main subject is placed off-center is often more pleasing.

The accompanying photograph illustrates this point. By composing the scene with the main subject (the child) off-center, I was able to include the red sign in my picture—adding color and interest to the photo. A tightly cropped photograph would not have been as interesting.

I used both creative composition and technical knowledge of photography to help communicate the feeling of a Hong Kong street. By using a 300mm telephoto lens, I was able to photograph the child from a distance without being noticed. Also, I used a medium-speed film, Kodachrome 200, which enabled me to hand-hold the camera at a shutter speed of 1/250 second.

If you have an autofocus 35mm SLR, you need to be careful when photographing off-center subjects. These cameras have sensors that help deliver sharp images of subjects in the center of the frame—which is where the autofocus sensor is located. With autofocus cameras there is a great tendency to just aim and shoot. However, most autofocus SLRs are equipped with

When composing a scene, some beginner photographers place the subject directly in the center of the frame. Professionals, on the other hand, often place the subject off-center and use creative composition to tell a more complete story.

(photo #12, page 56)

AF locks that enable you to lock focus on a subject and then recompose the scene.

In the photograph of the Chinese girl, you can see that the center of the scene is about two feet behind the subject. Autofocusing on this point would have produced a slightly out of focus subject.

If you are shooting in a situation like this with an autofocus camera, it would be best to prefocus—using the autofocus lock—on the main subject and then recompose before you shoot.

If you use an autofocus camera, remember this: For eye-catching photographs, rather than just snapshots, you must think before you shoot—one of the golden rules of photography.

Selective Focus

On a recent outing to the zoo, I was presented with a photographic challenge. I wanted a picture of a snowy owl to look as though it had been taken in the wilderness. However, it was obvious to the trained eye that the habitat had been built by humans, not to mention that the owl was behind row of wires. In addition, I wanted to get striking portraits of this interesting animal—portraits that had a three-dimensional effect.

To overcome the challenge and accomplish my goal I used a photographic technique called "selective focus," which produces a sharp subject and a blurred background or foreground.

Knowing that selecting large apertures on telephoto lenses results in shallow depth of field, I decided to shoot with a 300mm lens set at f/5.6 on my 35mm SLR camera. Looking through the viewfinder, I quickly saw I had made the correct shooting choice.

When you are in similar shooting situations, selective focus can make all the difference between a dramatic photograph and a snapshot. Remember, the background or foreground is just as important as the main subject, and you must be aware of how elements in these areas affect your picture.

Shooting with a telephoto lens set at a large f-stop also can blur the foreground. Therefore, if you are shooting through the bars or wire of a cage at a zoo, selective focus can blur these distracting foreground elements. In fact, it may blur

Good photographs don't always require total sharpness. In fact, selective focus is often preferred to highlight a subject and blur a distracting foreground or background.
(photo #13, page 56)

them to the extent that they disappear in your photograph.

Selective focus is also beneficial when photographing flowers and plants with a standard lens, where it's often difficult to compose a scene with a non-distracting background. Here, too, it's advisable to select a large f-stop for shallow depth of field.

When shooting with any lens, it's important to remember that camera-to-subject distance affects depth of field. After selecting an f-stop, the closer you get to a subject, the less depth of field you have. If you want to increase your depth of field, select a smaller f-stop or move farther away from your subject.

To take the guesswork out of what will be in focus and what will be out of focus, some 35mm SLRs have depth of field preview buttons. By pressing the preview button before you take a photograph, you see precisely how much of the scene will be in focus. Thus you'll have few surprises when your prints or slides are returned.

Dramatic Lighting: Mood Photos

A friend of mine says that one of the great things about photography is that people get an inner sense of peace and satisfaction when they take pictures, as well as when they see the results of their efforts.

I agree with this philosophy. However, I'd like to take that idea one step further. I've found that most photographers, amateurs and professionals alike, seem to revel in photographs that create a mood—those images that capture the true feeling of the moment.

For some picture-takers, this happens by accident. They just get lucky. For others, mood photographs are the result of evaluating the scene and then drawing on experience and knowledge to make precise exposure decisions.

For those readers who have felt "something" when looking through the viewfinder, but have been unable to capture this special feeling on film, here are a few easy-to-follow tips, tricks, and techniques:

Silhouettes. When photographing subjects against a much brighter background, such as a sky or shimmering water, you will get a silhouette if you set your camera on automatic. To increase the silhouette effect, underexpose the scene by setting the ISO dial to double the film's recommended ISO setting, or by setting the exposure compensation dial to the -1 position.

Dramatic lighting produces dramatic photographs. By slightly underexposing slide film, you can increase the color saturation of the recorded scene.
(photo #14, page 57)

Color shifts. You will get unexpected and dramatic color effects when using longer than normal exposures to photograph dawn and dusk scenes. These exposures can be up to several minutes long, which will require a slow film, a tripod, and perhaps a neutral-density filter, which reduces the amount of light entering the lens. The basic rule for long exposures is that the longer the shutter is open, the more dramatic the color shift.

Blurring action. Although today's cameras have super-fast shutter speeds, slow shutter speeds are sometimes preferred to create the effect of speed and motion. When photographing a fast-moving subject, experiment with slower shutter speeds, from 1/60 second down to one second. Again, a tripod is a useful accessory to steady the camera during long exposures.

High-speed films. High-speed films (ISO 400–1000) have more grain than slower films. The higher the speed, the more evident the grain. In addition, shooting in subdued lighting conditions will increase the apparent grain in a picture. However, grain can actually enhance a scene, especially when shooting with a soft-focus or fog filter.

Here's a final tip on how to create a mood photo: Stop and smell the roses. All too often, our fast-paced lives don't allow us to enjoy the beautiful sights we see. We pick up our camera, shoot, and move on to the next location. The next time you look through the viewfinder and see a great picture, take a deep breath, enjoy the moment, and try to feel the scene. If you get in the mood, this feeling will most likely be reflected in your picture.

Special Effects

In the early days of photography, when an amateur photographer saw a photo special effect, he or she was amazed that such an image could be created on film. Today, all photographers can easily create their own special effects photos—if they know a few tricks of the trade.

Special effect filters are a popular way to create one-of-a-kind effects. Here are just a few:

- **Star.** Turns points of light into starbursts.
- **Speed.** Creates a soft blur behind a subject.
- **Double exposure.** Blocks out half the frame for each exposure.
- **Binoculars.** A black cardboard cutout that creates the impression that the picture was taken through binoculars.
- **Five prism.** Turns a single subject into five identical subjects.
- **Colored polarizer.** Adds dramatic color (usually red or green) to a scene.
- **Rainbow.** Adds a rainbow to a clear sky.

Another way to create special effects is to use special films. Infra-red film, for example, will produce unusual and unpredictable effects when used with or without a filter—and at different ISO settings.

High-contrast film is also popular for creating special effects. This film does exactly what its name says it does: produce striking high-contrast pictures.

When you're trying to produce a special effect with a film or filter, bracketing is essential.

I used a Cokin speed filter to "increase" the speed of the motor boat in this picture. This is just one type of special effect photographers use to create original images.
(photo #15, page 57)

Sometimes, a filter can "fool" the camera's light meter. And when it comes to infra-red and high-contrast films, results are so unpredictable that taking different exposures is essential to ensure a good exposure or an acceptable special effect.

Zoom lenses also can be used to create a special effect nighttime photo. Set your camera on a tripod and set your lens at the longest focal length. Select a slow shutter speed, as long as one second. Then, immediately after you press the shutter release button, zoom to the widest setting. The results will be a dramatic picture with the lights streaking out toward the edge of your picture. Here, too, bracketing the shutter speed is important to ensure the desired effect.

Photo #1: *Composing for color in a photograph is just as important as composing for a subject. To emphasize the color in this Sicilian beach scene, I exposed Kodachrome 64 at ISO 80. The one-quarter stop underexposure provided a more dramatic saturation of the colors in the photo. I also used a polarizing filter on my 24mm lens to darken the sky.*

Photo #2 (left): *For me, a good photograph is one that captures a precious moment in time—such as the setting sun in Galapagos. To perfectly record this frigate bird in silhouette against the sun, I took seventy-two exposures. This is my favorite.*

Photo #3 (below): *The elements needed to make a good picture include an interesting subject, dependable camera equipment, film that can record the true color of your subject, practice, and last but not least, luck. This picture of a group of children surrounding my boat on an island in Indonesia is the result of all these elements coming together—especially luck! In situations like this I shoot on automatic because I'm interested in recording the moment, before it's gone.*

Photo #4: *Good photographs are the result of your interests, good technique, and the special way you see a subject. This child was part of a group of school children in Siberia. I used a 100mm lens to isolate him—my favorite subject—from the crowd.*

Photo #5 (top inset): *Different lenses are designed for different shooting situations. For this photo of a temple in Bali, I used a 24mm wide-angle lens for foreground-to-infinity sharpness. Framing the subject with tree branches added depth to the image.*
Photo #6 (bottom inset): *When shooting with an SLR camera, you can add accessories that expand your photographic horizons, such as a wide-angle lens for good depth of field and a polarizing filter to darken the sky.*

Photo #7: *As illustrated by this picture of a freighter on Siberia's Lake Baikal, a polarizing filter can reduce glare on water and brighten white clouds against a blue sky. Fine-grain film produces ultra-sharp pictures.*

Photo #8: *In-camera light meters make it relatively easy to get a good exposure when a scene is evenly lit. In tricky backlit lighting situations such as this one, however, bracketing is essential for a correct exposure. (Model: Karen Trella. Setting: Lake Powell, NV)*

Photo #9 (above left): *Sophisticated 35mm autofocusing SLR cameras provide fast focus in the majority of shooting situations. But in low-light situations, it may actually be faster to focus manually. I learned this when photographing this teacher in a school room in a remote Chinese village.* **Photo #10 (above right):** *Automatic exposure modes usually produce picture-perfect results. For this photo of a Native American boy in Monument Valley, I used the Program mode, which automatically selected and set the aperture and shutter speed for correct exposure. (Model: George Tooenapper)*

Photo #11 (left): *Zoom lenses give you flexibility over composition without having to change your position. This is a big advantage when you are locked into a shooting location, as I was when photographing Jimmy Carter during his speaking engagement in New York City. For this photo I used an 80–200mm zoom with the lens set at 200mm. Note how the photo loses impact if you cover Mr. Carter's hand.*

Photo #12 (above): *When composing a scene, some beginner photographers place the subject directly in the center of the frame. Professionals, on the other hand, often place the subject off-center and use creative composition to tell a more complete story.*

Photo #13 (left): *Good photographs don't always require total sharpness. In fact, selective focus is often preferred to highlight a subject and blur a distracting foreground or background. This photograph of a snowy owl actually was taken in a zoo.*

Photo #14 (left): *Dramatic lighting produces dramatic photographs. By slightly underexposing slide film, you can increase the color saturation of the recorded scene. For this dramatic silhouette, I exposed Ektachrome 50 film at ISO 64, with the camera set on automatic.*

Photo #15 (below): *I used a Cokin speed filter to "increase" the speed of the motor boat in this picture. This is just one type of special effect photographers use to create original images.*

Photo #16 (left): *By changing my position outside of the baboon exhibit at the Bronx Zoo, I was able to compose this picture of a baboon with a clean, black background. This put the entire focus of the photograph on my subject.*

Photo #17 (below): *These seventeenth- and eighteenth-century Dutch artifacts, recovered during an expedition to the island of St. Eustatius, were photographed with a 60mm macro lens against my favorite portable background for small objects—my T-shirt.*

Photo #18: *Getting the correct exposure when using slide film is sometimes tricky, especially when photographing dark subjects against light backgrounds (and vice versa). Bracketing one stop over and one stop under the recommended setting will help ensure a correctly exposed picture. You can also bracket in one-half stops and even one-quarter stops to fine-tune exposures.*

Photo #19 (top inset): *As illustrated in this photo of a Galapagos blue-footed booby, an on-camera flash can fill in harsh shadows caused by direct sunlight. It's also a useful accessory outdoors when light levels are too low for hand-held picture-taking. When I'm on wildlife photo assignments I always pack a flash.*

Photo #20 (bottom inset): *Understanding how light affects film is one of the basic elements of photography. On overcast days, for example, diffused sunlight lets you take shadowless pictures.*

Photo #21: *Exposure meters in some automatic cameras can be "fooled" by high contrast scenes, like this flock of flamingos resting in the shade. In situations like this, you can get an accurate exposure by bracketing, using a hand-held spot meter to take a reading of the light reflected from the subject, or using a hand-held incident light meter to read the light falling on the subject.*

Photo #22: *If you're like most dedicated photography enthusiasts, you'll make plenty of mistakes on the road to becoming a good photographer. I certainly did! Analyzing your mistakes, and seeing how to avoid them, helps you prepare for fleeting photographic moments, like these three boys posing briefly for me in a remote village in Indonesia.*

Photo #23 (top inset): *Good vacation photos help you relive fond memories and share your adventures with others. When you travel, pack plenty of extra film and batteries.*
Photo #24 (bottom inset): *As a travel photographer I often encounter dimly lit indoor subjects, such as this altar in a Hong Kong temple. To get good low-light pictures, I use ISO 200 or 400 film and a fast (f/2.8) wide-angle lens.*

Photo #25: *Photographing small sections of large subjects with a macro lens can produce interesting abstract images, such as this ice and snow patch on Lake Baikal.*

Photo #26: *Most photographers use wide-angle lenses for landscape photography. However, as this photograph of the German countryside illustrates, a 200mm telephoto lens also can produce pleasing results by compressing the elements in the scene.*

The All-Important Background

Fully automatic 35mm AF SLR cameras make it easy for first-time photographers to do exactly what the camera manufacturers suggest: simply point and shoot. But perhaps the most common mistake beginner photographers make is to overlook the importance of the background. I've seen countless photos in which trees, signs or light poles seem to be "growing" out of the subject's head. Another common mistake is placing the subject against a distracting background, such as a building with intricate lines or patterns.

Whenever I shoot, indoors or out, one of the first things I consider is the background: Will it enhance the photograph? If not, I use a telephoto lens and shoot tight, which all but eliminates the background, or I select a wide aperture for shallow depth of field.

However, if the background will add to the beauty of the scene, I spend time viewing the scene from different positions. When shooting portraits, I test different wide-angle lenses and semi-wide-angle lenses to see which one will provide the best composition and subject-to-background ratio. Not until I have an idea of what I want to accomplish do I ask the subject to step in. By working in this manner, I can shoot fast, without making my subject feel uncomfortable.

By changing my position, I was able to compose this picture of a baboon with a clean, black background. This put the entire focus of the photograph on my subject.
(photo #16, page 58)

Close-Ups

I photographed these Dutch artifacts with a 60mm macro lens and my favorite portable background for small objects—my T-shirt. (photo #17, page 58)

Taking close-up photographs opens up a whole new world of creativity for photographers. When subjects are photographed life-size or larger-than-life-size, their fine details have a strong impact on our visual senses.

Flowers, insects, jewelry, and sea shells are idea subjects for close-up photographs. To capture their beauty and detail on film with a 35mm AF SLR camera, three accessories are available: a close-up attachment, a macro lens, and a bellows unit.

Close-up attachments. If you are on a tight budget, have a lens with a focal length between 35mm and 55mm lens, and are new to picture-taking, the least expensive way to get into close-up photography is to purchase a set of inexpensive close-up lenses. These lenses, which screw onto the front element of your lens, are actually filters that are designed to work with SLR lenses with focal lengths from 35mm to 55mm. They are available in three magnifications: 0.7x, 1.5x, and 3x.

For greater magnification, close-up attachments can be stacked together, but with a resulting loss in picture quality.

Macro lenses. Most 35mm AF SLR camera manufacturers offer autofocus macro lenses for their cameras. Focal lengths vary from company to company. Some offer 50mm and 105mm lenses, while another may offer 55mm and

105mm lenses.

Macro lenses produce a range of magnifications, including life-size reproduction. This versatility makes a macro lens a creative tool for the serious photographer.

Macro lenses also function as non-macro lenses of the same focal length. This means you can use a 50mm macro lens for general picture-taking, and a 105mm macro lens for portraiture and other types of telephoto photography.

The versatility macro lenses offer does not come cheap. In most cases, a macro lens is several times more expensive than a non-macro lens of the same focal length.

Bellows. If you are very serious about taking extreme close-ups of small subject, there are a variety of bellows units available. Bellows units mount on a tripod and fit between your camera and a 50mm lens (which can be mounted backwards for even greater magnification).

By adjusting the length of the bellows, you can "dial in" the precise amount of magnification you want.

Bellows units are less expensive than macro lenses, but they do require setting up a tripod and "working" on your photograph—which is good training in composition.

Bracketing for Proper Exposure

Getting the correct exposure when using slide film is sometimes tricky. Bracketing exposures will help ensure a correctly exposed picture.
(photo #18, page 59)

While reading through a photography magazine, I noticed that many photographic manufacturers use two terms when promoting their 35mm automatic cameras: *automatic exposure* and *point-and-shoot simplicity*. In fairness to the manufacturers, their cameras do deliver good results, automatically, in the majority of outdoor shooting situations. However, there are times when a little extra attention to detail is required if you want to get a correctly exposed picture.

The easiest way to ensure a correctly exposed picture is to "bracket" your exposures. This is a technique by which you take a picture at the recommended exposure setting, and then take additional pictures over and under that setting.

If you shoot slide film and want a perfectly exposed picture, I highly recommend bracketing your exposures. This is necessary because slide film has what's called a narrow exposure latitude, which means your exposure must be "right on." Negative (print) film, on the other hand, has a wide exposure latitude, so you will still get a good print even if you slightly overexpose or underexpose the negative.

Bracketing is recommended when you have a dark subject against a light background, such as a red brick building against a sky filled with white clouds, or a child with a deep tan on a white sandy beach. The opposite also is true: Bracketing is a good idea if you are

white boat on a deep blue lake or a girl in a white dress under the shade of tree.

With an automatic SLR, there are several ways to bracket, which is why these cameras are the choice of professional photographers who must get the shot each and every time. Most SLRs have +/- exposure compensation controls, which let you dial in the desired exposure compensation. Sophisticated camera models let you do this in one-quarter stops and up to several stops in both directions. But if that's not good enough, several camera manufacturers offer accessory SLR camera backs that, when set accordingly, automatically program the camera to take up to nine different exposures of the same scene.

Bracketing on an automatic SLR also can be accomplished via the camera's ISO (film speed) dial. If you are shooting ISO 100 film, for example, setting the dial on 200 will give you an exposure one stop under the recommended setting; on 50 you will get an exposure one stop over the setting that the camera is recommending.

Most automatic 35mm fixed-lens cameras don't have bracketing capabilities. However, many do have backlight compensation buttons, which, when pressed, adjust the exposure accordingly for backlit subjects. Some models also feature auto/manual fill-flash, which compensates for situations like the aforementioned scene of the girl in the shade.

If you've been disappointed with your pictures, either because they were too dark or too light, bracketing probably will improve your results. If you're thinking about buying a camera, ask your photo dealer about its bracketing capabilities before you make your purchase, especially if you plan to shoot slide film.

One final note about bracketing. True, you will take more pictures and your film and developing costs will increase. However, it's important to keep in mind that these costs are the least expensive elements of recording your memories—especially if you have spent a good deal of money getting to an exotic vacation destination.

Seeing and Recording Light

Learning how to see light is one of the key elements in taking good photographs. After all, light is the most important element in a photograph; without it, the image would be black. As one professional photographer put it, "We don't photograph objects, we photograph light."

When photographers talk about seeing light, they are talking about subject brightness, contrast, and the quality (strong or soft) of light. All of these elements effect an image, often producing unexpected results on film. Why? Because our eyes see the world one way, and our cameras and film quite often another. For example, when we view a mountainous landscape at sunrise or sunset, filled with deep shadows, brightly illuminated meadows, and a bright, cloud-filled sky, we can see detail in all the aforementioned elements.

However, if we photograph this scene with an automatic camera, some of the elements may be too dark to distinguish (shadow areas) or washed out (sky). The picture may be pleasing to some, but would not represent the broad spectrum of light the eye sees. (I don't often get philosophical, but photography does give one a much greater appreciation for the wonderful gift of sight.)

So the question is this: How do we get accurate photographs of what we see? Fortunately, we have a few options that can help us with this challenge. Bracketing (taking exposures one

Understanding how light affects film is one of the basic elements of photography. On overcast days, for example, diffused sunlight lets you take shadowless pictures. (photo #20, page 60)

stop over and one stop under the recommended reading) produces slightly different results of your subject, lightening some areas while darkening others. A graduated neutral density filter, which darkens approximately half the frame, can be used to reduce contrast in a scene.

Another important element in capturing light is film selection. Color print film has a greater exposure latitude than slide film, which means subjects can be slightly over or underexposed and you'll still get a good image. When shooting slides, it's advisable to meter (expose for) the brightest portion of scene, because overexposed subjects usually are more displeasing than subjects that are underexposed.

Speaking of metering, some cameras have built-in spot meters to help you determine the correct exposure for a subject. However, if you really want to get serious about metering, a hand-held spot meter, which reads only a very small portion of a subject, can determine subject brightness from great distances.

I've found the key to getting beautifully lit photographs, no matter what film, filter, or camera I use, is to experiment with bracketing, because who's to say what's the best lighting effect?

Patience and timing are other important elements in getting beautifully lit photographs. If you shoot in the early morning or late afternoon, you'll catch the soft, beautiful light of these special times of day; you'll also get warmer, more pleasing colors in your slides and prints. And be patient. During these hours, the quality of light changes quite rapidly, so you may get quite different effects and colors from moment to moment.

High Contrast Scenes

Camera manufacturers spend lots of time and money on research and development to design built-in camera meters that will deliver good exposures in average shooting situations. If your scene has relatively low contrast and is evenly illuminated, you will get a properly exposed picture when shooting in the automatic mode.

In a high contrast scene, such as a white bird against a dark background, your main subject may be overexposed. Conversely, if your subject is a black bear on white snow, the bear may be underexposed.

To get a proper exposure of your subject, you first need to "see" the contrast in the scene. This is fairly simple. View the scene in the viewfinder and ask yourself the following questions: Are there areas that are twice or more than twice as bright as others? Is my subject much lighter or much darker then the surrounding area? If the answer to one or both of these questions is yes, you need to either fill the entire frame with your main subject or adjust your exposure.

Adjusting the exposure can be accomplished in several ways. If you can get close to your subject, take a close-up meter reading with your camera set on automatic, then set your manual exposure controls to this setting, and move back to your original position to take the picture.

If you can't get close to the subject, take a

Exposure meters in some automatic cameras can be "fooled" by high contrast scenes. In situations like this, you can get an accurate exposure by bracketing, using a spot meter, or using an incident light meter. (photo #21, page 61)

reading of the light falling on the palm of your hand and set the camera accordingly. Another way to adjust exposure is to use the exposure +/- compensation dial: When using slide film, take photos at one-half-stop increments from one stop over to one stop under the recommended setting; with color print film this is not really necessary because print film has a greater exposure latitude than color slide film and will give you a good exposure even when photographing high contrast scenes — to a degree.

You also can control contrast with graduated neutral density filters. These filters do not add color to a scene but block out some of the light — either at the top or bottom of the frame — reaching the film. When the sky is two stops brighter than a field, for example, a one-half neutral density filter in the upper position will even out the light reaching the film. When the foreground is brighter than the sky, such as in snow scenes, turning the filter to the down position with help you get an evenly exposed picture.

Another way to adjust the exposure is to add artificial light with an on-camera flash, even when shooting outdoors. A daylight fill-in flash unit can compress the contrast ratio of a scene, giving you a better chance of getting properly exposed picture—automatically.

Daylight Fill-in Flash

Have you ever seen one of those behind-the-scenes documentaries that show how movies are made? If so, you have probably noticed all that fancy lighting equipment directors use to make actors look good.

Professional portrait photographers also use a myriad of expensive lighting gear—off-camera strobes, reflectors, and diffusers—to get professional-quality results.

Does this mean you have to make a major investment and commitment in fancy lighting equipment to get professional looking outdoor flash pictures with your 35mm camera? Not at all. Today's major 35mm autofocus SLR camera manufacturers all offer on-camera or in-camera flashes that produce automatic daylight fill-in flash pictures. In most cases, all you have to do is turn on the flash, compose, and shoot.

I use automatic daylight fill-in flash not only for outdoor portraits, but for outdoor animal and flower pictures, as well. On bright days, when the sun casts harsh shadows on my subject's face, I use a flash to fill in the shadows. On overcast days, when details are softened, I sometimes use a flash to make my pictures "pop." And when my subject is backlit, I use daylight fill-in flash to prevent a silhouette.

Some on-camera flash units offer variable automatic flash output, giving you a degree of creativity in your daylight flash pictures. Canon, for example, offers the EZ Speedlight for its

An on-camera flash can fill in harsh shadows caused by direct sunlight. It's also a useful accessory outdoors when light levels are too low for hand-held picture taking. (photo #19, page 60)

EOS-1 autofocus SLR. This marvel of ingenuity lets you vary the automatic light output from one stop over to three stops under the normal setting—at the touch of a button. There is no guesswork involved. The advantage to using a variable power flash is that you can add just the amount of light you want: more light for a brighter subject, less light for a more natural looking daylight/flash picture.

I've found that using a -1 or -2 setting on the flash gives me the most pleasing outdoor flash pictures—just the right mix of daylight and fill-in flash to produce a very natural looking photograph. For me, the "correct" or "normal" setting produces just a touch too much light, producing a picture that was obviously taken with the aid of a flash. You may feel differently. Therefore, I recommend bracketing your daylight fill-in flash pictures to see which setting is most pleasing to you.

To soften the effect of using a flash outdoors, try using a flash diffuser. These inexpensive accessories attach to flash units with velcro and produce a very soft flash effect.

I admit, I've made daylight fill-in flash photography with 35mm autofocus SLRs sound easy as pie. For most of your outdoor photos, this is indeed the case. However, if you want to get very serious about using daylight fill-in flash, I'd suggest asking your local dealer or camera manufacturer for flash system advice. You will learn about highly accurate hand-held flash meters, creative and corrective filters, flash head diffusers, and lighting ratios for two or more flash units.

If you can't be bothered with on-camera flash units and sophisticated flash accessories, but like the idea of daylight fill-in flash, I'd rec-

ommend using a simple 35mm lens-shutter camera. Here you have many models from which to
choose. Some even turn on the flash automatically when it's needed. Others fire a pre-expo-
sure flash that actually helps reduce the most
dreaded element in flash pictures: red eye.

Low-Light
Situations

*As a travel photogra-
pher I often encounter
dimly lit indoor sub-
jects. To get good low-
light pictures, I use ISO
200 or 400 film and a
fast (f/2.8) wide-angle
lens.*
(photo #24, page 63)

One of the most important recent advances in photography has been the development of high-quality low-light films, also known as superfast films. For the traveling photographer, these films offer new possibilities for capturing the true feeling, and soft existing lighting, of indoor settings. They enable you to shoot indoors without an on-camera flash, which can cause harsh lighting if fired directly toward the subject.

Several superfast slide and print films have recently been introduced. However, each film has its own distinctive color and grain character, and you should experiment to see which film suits your shooting preference.

For pictures in extremely dimly lit areas, such as the vestibule of an old English church, you may want to shoot with an ultra-fast film such as Kodak's Ektapress 1600 color print film.

If you get into a situation where your camera is telling you that it's still too dark and you need to use a flash, you still have a few choices. Obviously, you can use a flash. But before you do, you can "push" your slide film—set your camera at a film speed setting higher than the film's ISO number—and still get acceptable results. In most cases, you can at least double the film speed; that is, push ISO 100 to 200 or ISO 200 to 400. To determine the pushing limit of the film you are using, contact your local dealer or film manufacturer.

When you push a film, you must tell the

film processor at what speed it was exposed. If you don't, your prints or slides will be delivered over- or underexposed.

In addition to fast film, a 28mm or 24mm fixed focal length wide-angle lens is helpful when shooting indoors. Most wide-angle lenses have a maximum aperture of $f/1.7$ or $f/2.8$. These relatively wide openings let lots of light into your camera in a short period of time, enabling you to hand-hold your camera indoors while using a shutter speed fast enough to stop camera shake. Zoom lenses, on the other hand, often have a maximum aperture of $f/3.5$ or $f/4.5$. This reduction in the amount of light entering the camera requires a slower shutter speed, which dictates the use of a tripod or a flash.

There is one more important element to consider when shooting indoors in low light situations: color. If daylight is the main light source, you will have no problem in getting correct subject color with the aforementioned films. Things start to get tricky when daylight is mixed with artificial lighting, or when artificial lighting is the main source of illumination. In situations like this, you may need to use a color correction (CC) filter.

If you are a fanatic about getting correct color, not just close but exact, you'll need a color meter to determine which filters are needed in mixed lighting situations. Here again, your friendly photo dealer can assist you in selecting a meter that fits not only your needs, but your budget as well.

Abstract Images: Textures, Shapes and Colors

Photographing small sections of large subjects with a macro lens can produce interesting abstract images. (photo #25, page 64)

When looking through a camera's viewfinder, most of us try to photograph a "main" subject. We see the "big picture," and don't often notice the interesting, smaller details before our eyes.

When photographed correctly, small sections of a large subject can become dramatic abstract images—images that may even have more impact than a picture of the entire subject. For example, a picture of a tree may be pleasing, but an ultra-close-up of a back-lit leaf or the side-lit bark may be even more eye catching.

Here are a few more examples of the possibilities abstract images offer:

• A beach scene may be pleasing, but a telephoto view of shadows on the dunes may be more dramatic.

• A seascape photograph may capture the beauty of the scene, but a tight shot of sunlight reflecting off the waves could stir the imagination even more.

• A building may make a great architectural photograph, but a close-up of the lines and shapes on the building's facade may produce a much more graphic image.

Abstract images are everywhere. Capturing them in photos requires two things: a macro or telephoto lens to isolate a section of the main subject, and a good eye. The lens is the easy part. Training your eye to see abstract images takes practice.

The best way to develop an eye for abstract images is to constantly be on the lookout for them—even when you are not photographing. Then, when shooting, experiment with different angles and compositions to see which abstract images are most pleasing to your eye.

Avoiding Photo Faux Pas

If you're like most dedicated photography enthusiasts, you'll make plenty of mistakes on the road to becoming a good photographer. Analyzing your mistakes, and seeing how to avoid them, helps you prepare for fleeting photographic moments.
(photo #22, page 62)

Making mistakes is part of learning how to take good photographs. If you have ever misloaded your camera, forgotten to change the ISO rating, or gone out on a shoot with dead batteries, you know how frustrating it is to ruin a picture. However, I bet you've never made the same mistake twice.

I've made all the aforementioned common mistakes, as well as the following not so common errors. All have made me a better photographer.

On a jaunt to Hong Kong, I shot approximately sixty rolls of film. When I had the film processed, one roll came back with a curved black line across the top of each frame. Evidently, a hair had fallen into the camera body near the film plane. Now, I always check the interior of my camera when I load each and every roll of film.

One winter night, I wanted to photograph the skyline of Manhattan from a bridge in Queens. I composed the scene with the full moon at the top of the frame and a small camp-fire at the bottom. I thought I had a perfect picture. The next day, I sent the slides in for processing. Unfortunately, the automatic slide cutter, which reads the light and dark areas of slides to determine where to cut the frame, mistakenly read the dark, center portion of the scene as the edge of the frame. The result: All my slides were cut approximately in half. Now, in situations like this, where the edge of the frame may not be clear to the mechanical slide film cutter, I ask for processing only—no mounting.

Another bad film experience happened the following summer. To keep my film fresh, I had stored it in my freezer. When I saw a beautiful blue jay in my backyard, I took out a roll of film, loaded it in my camera, and shot away. When my film was returned, each frame was spotted. When the cold film was exposed to the warm air, condensation formed on the emulsion, resulting in spots. Now, I let frozen film "defrost" for several hours before I use it.

Another time I was shooting a beautiful sunset with a 28mm lens. I was using a lens shade, which screws into the front of a lens and prevents side or top light from reaching the lens's front element, reducing the possibility of lens flare. I thought I had an award-winning picture. However, when I viewed my slides, all four corners were blacked out. My mistake? I had used a 50mm lens shade on my 28mm lens, which cut into the field of view. Now I'm more careful when I'm doing simple photographic tasks — including screwing in lookalike lens shades.

Part 3:
Outdoors & Travel
Photography

Vacation Photos

Vacation time. The time of year most of you will pack your jeans, T-shirts, and sporting gear, and depart for popular vacation destinations around the globe.

Because you love photography, you may be anxious to pack your gear and get on the road. However, before you leave home, there are some important points to consider if you want to get good pictures.

Let's start with the basics. First of all, if you have not used your camera in the past few months, it's a good idea to change the batteries. Dead batteries in locations where there is no corner drug store means no pictures. I also recommend taking a cloth to your camera and giving it some TLC. Dust and grime can adversely affect your camera's controls, so a once-over is well worthwhile.

Film should be the next item on your checklist. Most vacationers overshoot, and wind up having to buy film (at a higher price) on location. Therefore, try to estimate how much shooting you'll be doing, and double it. If worse comes to worse, you can always bring the film back home.

I'm often asked if airport X-ray machines damage film. My reply is, "Better safe than sorry. Always have your film hand-checked." Although the X-ray machines are not supposed to fog (slightly expose) film, there is a chance that the machine may be out of calibration. When it comes to your valuable (and expensive)

Good vacation photos help you relive fond memories and share your adventures with others. When you travel, pack plenty of extra film and batteries. (photo #23, page 63)

memories, it's worth the inconvenience to ask the security guard to hand-check your camera bag. Don't take no for an answer. If you do want to put your film through the X-ray machine, you must place it in a special lead-lined pouch, available at most camera stores. This inexpensive X-ray–proof pouch will protect your film, as long as it doesn't have a hole or tear in it.

If you plan to travel to a foreign country, I strongly recommend that you register all your camera gear at the airport customs office before you leave. If you don't, you may have to pay duty on your own equipment when you return home.

Once you get to your destination, keep your camera handy. This may sound like a simple procedure, but many people tuck their cameras neatly away in a camera bag and miss those once-in-a-lifetime shots that happen in the blink of an eye.

My favorite vacation photos are those of people. Often, a close-up of a face captures the expression not only of the individual, but of the country as well. For people photography, I suggest following three basic rules: Be friendly, ask permission to take a picture, and say thank you.

There are two kinds of people photos: portraits and environmental shots. For portraits, get as close as possible. "The name of the game is to fill the frame" is a good rule to follow. For environmental photos, move back, and include some of the surrounding area in the picture. These pictures will tell a story and put the viewer in the scene.

For both types of people shots, I like to use automatic fill-in flash (available on most point-and-shoot and SLR cameras). By using a flash in daylight, you'll brighten up your subject's face, especially the eyes.

Landscapes and cityscapes should be included in your personal photo travelogue. The main guidelines here are to keep the horizon line level and to shoot with an object (tree, railing, fence, etc.) in the foreground. This will add depth and dimension to your picture, giving those who view it a reference point.

Finally, one of the main ingredients for good vacation pictures is color. If you shoot in the early morning or late afternoon hours, you'll get pleasing pictures with a "warmer" tone. You'll also avoid harsh shadows caused by direct overhead sunlight. It's worth the extra effort to plan your day so you're in a good location for sunrise and sunset. These pictures will undoubtedly be among the favorites in your photo album or slide show, and will bring back the very special feeling of traveling—a wanderlust that we all share.

Landscapes

Most photographers use wide-angle lenses for landscape photography. But a 200mm telephoto lens also can produce pleasing results by compressing the elements in the scene.
(photo# 26, page 64)

When building a lens system, most photographers choose a wide-angle lens (20mm–28mm) for landscape photography. It's a good choice: Wide-angle lenses, when stopped down to small f-stops, deliver good depth of field. In fact, when a 24mm wide-angle lens is set at f/16, the entire scene—from two feet in front of the camera to infinity—will be in focus. However, telephoto lenses also can be effective for landscape photography.

Telephoto lenses are most effective in landscape photography when you want to isolate an area of the scene or "compress" the different elements in a scene. Telephoto lenses also are useful when the foreground is detracting or distracting from your picture.

No matter what lens you choose for landscape photography, the following guidelines should help you get good pictures.

Composition. One of the basic rules of photography is to never cut the frame in half with the horizon line. Most often, this is a good rule to follow, especially when the sky is overcast or clear blue, leaving lots of "dead space" in your picture. However, when the sky is filled with beautiful blue clouds, include them in your picture, even if you have to break the aforementioned composition rule.

Before you shoot, frame the scene with the horizon line in different areas, and choose the position that you like the best.

Filters. Creative and corrective filters play an important part in landscape photography. First, always use a polarizing filter when the sun is shining. This filter will reduce reflection on ponds and lakes, "cut through" atmospheric haze, and darken white clouds against a blue sky. In addition, a polarizing filter will reduce reflections on moist trees and grass when you are shooting on a sunny day. This reduction of reflections will give your picture more "snap" and color.

Graduated filters also are useful. These filters generally are half-clear and half-colored— with the color starting at the center of the frame and becoming gradually darker toward one side. Graduated filers are available in a wide range of colors, from blue to pastels. There are even sunset filters that turn a noonday scene into a sunset scene. When you want to add or change the color of the sky, these filters will do the trick.

A skylight filter (or haze filter) also will reduce the effect of haze on film. These filters are relatively inexpensive and, in addition to reducing haze, will reduce your repair bill in case you accidentally knock the expensive front element of your lens.

Tripod. Famous photographers such as Ansel Adams have been known to spend hours setting up just one landscape photo. They wait for exactly the right light, and in most cases, have their cameras on tripods so they can make an exposure at just the right moment.

A tripod serves another purpose: It gives you the opportunity to concentrate on the subject at hand. When the camera is set atop a tripod, you can examine every element in the scene, from the foreground to infinity. You may be surprised at just how much you'll notice once your camera is securely mounted in place.

Blurring Water

Long exposures (1/30 second to several seconds) are necessary to capture the beauty of flowing water.
(photo #27, page 145)

Whether you are photographing Niagara Falls or a small waterfall along the local stream, careful attention must be paid to the shutter speed at which you are shooting.

Fast shutter speeds "freeze" water droplets in motion, producing pictures in which the water does not look natural. Slow shutter speeds, on the other hand, blur flowing water, creating a more natural-looking picture.

Generally speaking, shutter speeds of less than 1/30 second will produce pleasing results. The slower the shutter speed, the more the water will appear blurred.

You can get a slow shutter speed in several ways:

• With your camera set in the Aperture Priority Mode (or adjustable Program Mode), adjust the f-stop until you see a slow shutter speed in the camera's viewfinder.

• On sunny days, use a slow film, such as Kodachrome 25. Slow films are less sensitive to light than medium speed and fast films and require longer exposures.

• If your favorite film has an ISO rating of 100 or higher, use a neutral-density filter to reduce the amount of light entering the lens.

• When you don't have slow film or a neutral density filter, shoot before dawn or after sunset. The low light levels at these hours require slow shutter speeds.

When shooting at slow shutter speeds, a tripod or other camera support is required to steady the camera to prevent camera shake. Remember: When photographing water, you want the water blurred and the surrounding scenery sharp.

By experimenting with different shutter speeds when photographing waterfalls, you'll get a picture on film that you've seen in your "mind's eye."

Shooting in the Snow

It was below zero when I took this photograph of a Russian caravan on Lake Baikal. Right until the moment of exposure, I kept my camera inside my warm coat— where my body heat helped to keep the camera's battery "alive." (photo #29, page 147)

Shooting in the snow presents many photographic opportunities. For example, a landscape covered with snow, especially at early morning or late afternoon, looks like a winter wonderland. A pond covered with snow and ice takes on an entirely different personality than the same pond in summer or fall. And family winter sports activities—skiing, ice skating, and sleigh riding—bring back "warm" memories of good times spent together.

Shooting in the snow requires certain precautions. Flexible plastic camera bags are available for virtually all 35mm cameras. These bags are sealed and have optical ports that won't affect image sharpness. An alternative to buying these bags is placing your camera in a plastic sandwich bag, leaving a hole for the lens. This technique will protect your camera from falling snow, but that's about it.

When it's very cold outside, it's advisable to keep your camera zipped inside your coat until you are ready to shoot. This will keep the camera batteries warm and prevent them from draining due to the cold. If you have an automatic camera and your batteries do die, you will not be able to fire the shutter (unless you have a manual mode, and even then your camera's light meter will not work.) If you plan to be outside all day, it's also advisable to keep an extra battery inside your coat.

Cold temperatures make film brittle, and

the colder the temperature, the more brittle the film. If you are used to shooting with a high-speed motor drive, don't use it when it comes to shooting in the snow when it's below zero. The speed may snap the film. Use the manual film advance instead.

Motor drives, by running the film though the camera at high speeds, can create static electricity on your film, which will look like lightening bolts in your pictures. Some cameras have special film pressure plates that help reduce static electricity buildup and motor drives that run at a speed that probably will not damage your film when shooting in cold conditions.

Snow has a tendency to have a blue tint on film if photographed without a skylight filter. Therefore, you should use this inexpensive filter at all times when snow shooting.

A polarizing filter is also useful for snow shooting. It will eliminate the sun's glare on snow and ice. However, glare sometimes adds to a scene, so don't be too quick to eliminate it.

When the sun is shining, you can use slow to medium speed film (ISO 50–100) to record your day in the snow. If you use a fast film in the ISO 400–1000 range, your camera may not be able to deliver a small enough f-stop/shutter speed combination for a proper exposure. In this case, your pictures will be overexposed.

Remember, if you are shooting with an SLR in the automatic exposure mode, it's important to note the following: Bright snow (and beach) scenes can fool a camera's meter into thinking that the scene is brighter than it actually is. To avoid getting an underexposed picture, over-expose the scene by one-half or one stop using either the ISO dial or +/- exposure compensation dial.

Sand and Sun

Beach photography presents lots of high-contrast situations. A dark subject on a bright, sandy background can fool your camera's meter, and thus requires a careful, close-up meter reading of the subject before you make an exposure. (photo #30, page 147)

A day at the beach is filled with picture-taking opportunities. At sunrise, you can photograph fishermen casting for a tasty meal, sea gulls gliding on air currents, and joggers out for their morning exercise. You can shoot with the sun behind you to get photos full of detail. Or, you can shoot with the sun behind the subject to make dramatic silhouettes.

Around midday, when the light is at its brightest, you can get great close-up shots of shells, crabs, and rocks. You also can be creative with filters to produce a wide variety of effects. Remember that when shooting on automatic at the beach, the bright sand and sun can fool your camera's meter and may cause you to take underexposed pictures; try slightly overexposing the scene.

The beautiful low lighting of late afternoon is ideal for portraiture and glamour photography. This also is a good time for taking pictures of family, friends, and fellow beachgoers having a great time. You can photograph them in or out of the water.

Just before sunset, when the low sun creates dramatic shadows, you can capture interesting patterns and textures in the sand.

All these shooting situations have a positive effect on most photographers. However, they can have a negative effect on delicate camera gear. Sand, salt spray, and heat are not your camera's best friends.

The simplest way to protect your camera is

to keep it in a camera case when it's not in use. When you are shooting, keep the camera in a plastic bag with a hole cut out for the lens. If you want to fully protect your camera, flexible plastic housings that feature hard, optical plastic ports should be used. These housings, available at most camera dealers, can even be used for shooting in the water and under water to depths of 150 feet.

If you don't want to take your expensive SLR or lens-shutter camera to the beach, where it may be damaged or stolen, Kodak and Fuji offer inexpensive one-use cameras. These splash-proof point-and-shoot cameras deliver relatively good images and are ideal for taking snapshots that capture the fun and action of a day at the beach.

If you're very serious about getting great beach photos, you'll need a selection of filters. A polarizing filter is perhaps the most useful filter at the beach. It can darken the blue sky, reduce reflection from the water and glare from the sand, and increase color saturation.

A skylight filter is also helpful. It reduces the blue cast caused by ultraviolet (UV) light radiation present in most beach scenes. (Film in inherently sensitive to UV.) The slight pink color of the skylight filter also helps to keep flesh tones looking natural by removing the excess blue.

Creative filters are also helpful, and fun to use, at the beach. You might experiment with a fog filter, which gives sunlit scenes a misty appearance; or a half-blue, half-clear graduated filter, which turns a gray sky into a blue sky. There also are sunset filters, which transform a midday setting into a sunset scene, and star filters, which cause intense points of light to record as stars.

I have two final recommendations for dedicated beach photographers. The first is to shoot with a slow film in the ISO 25–50 range. Due to the bright light level, you'll need this film for greater shutter speed and *f*-stop flexibility when shooting on manual. These films also give you pictures with very little grain. The second recommendation is to take along a telephoto lens or a telephoto zoom. The long focal length enables you to get candid close-ups of children playing in the sand and water.

Sunsets

A setting sun can fill the sky with beautiful shades of red, pink, orange, and yellow. It can create dramatic shadows and silhouettes. And, it can inspire photographers to try to capture a once-in-a-lifetime moment on film.

However, photographing sunsets can be a bit tricky. Oftentimes, sunset pictures do not turn out as they had been envisioned by the photographer. If you have been disappointed with the results of your sunset shots, or plan to capture a setting sun on your next vacation, the following tips may prove useful.

Use color slide film as opposed to color print film. Under normal exposure conditions, slide films produce an accurate rendition of what you see. However, if you use long exposures (longer than one second), most slide films will produce surprising, pleasing color shifts. Pictures taken with color print film, on the other hand, may be "color corrected" in the lab to the technician's and machine's liking—so what you see in your initial proofs may not be what you expected. But there is hope here, too. If you don't like the colors in your pictures, take them back to the lab for a redo, which most likely will be done free of charge.

Since you'll be shooting toward the setting sun, your scene will have a very wide exposure range, from the bright sun and sky to the darker foreground. The key to getting a properly exposed picture is to bracket your exposure.

The most dramatic colors of sunsets are of-

Sunsets are one of the most photogenic—and most photographed—subjects. To capture the true beauty of the setting sun, you'll need to bracket your exposures. And don't always place the sun in the dead center of the scene. (photo #28, page 146)

ten seen after the sun drops below the horizon. In this reduced lighting situation, you will be shooting at slow shutter speeds—which could cause a blurry picture due to camera shake. For steady pictures, pack a tripod or other camera support.

If you plan to shoot after sundown, use a film that has an ISO rating of 200 or 400. These films are more sensitive to light than slower films are (ISO 50 and 100) and will help you capture the fleeting colors in the sky.

Compose your scene with care. Use foreground elements, such as trees and fences, to add depth to your scene. When shooting into the sunset, these elements will be dramatically silhouetted.

Experiment with filters. Red, orange, and yellow filters can intensify the colors of a sunset, or even add color when it's absent. A sunset filter can even turn an overcast, midday scene into a dramatic sunset—just imagine what it will do to a real life sunset.

One final, and important, tip: Don't always place the sun (main subject) in the center of the frame. Use creative composition to position the horizon line and setting sun for a more dramatic effect.

Shooting After Dark

Whenever I travel to a foreign city, I always make a point to photograph the city at night. After the sun sets, the mood and feeling of a city changes completely. This is when many cities "come alive" with the color and drama of neon signs and the action of streaking headlights and taillights.

Photographing nighttime scenes is exciting, rewarding, and, like all tricky photographic situations, challenging. For those of you who would like to accept the challenge, here are a few basic tips and techniques.

Choosing a film is the first, and perhaps most important, step. Since nighttime scenes are often a mixture of different kinds of illuminations—tungsten lights, neon signs, fluorescent bulbs, sodium vapor lamps, headlights, taillights, and even daylight when shooting at dusk—daylight balanced films or tungsten films will produce acceptable results. I prefer to shoot daylight balanced slide films because I like the "warm" tones they produce. (Tungsten films produce cooler images, which some folks prefer.)

Films in the ISO 200–400 range are well suited for nighttime photography. If you are shooting with a fast lens (f/2.8) in a fairly bright setting, a fast film may enable you to shoot at a hand-holdable shutter speed. However, most of the time you'll be shooting at relatively slow shutter speeds, which dictate the use of a tripod, unipod or other camera support.

Getting the correct exposure is the main

After sunset, you can create striking graphic images of illuminated buildings—if you have a fast film (ISO 200 or 400) and a tripod. (photo #31, page 147)

99

challenge in nighttime photography. For your first-time nighttime shooting session, take a reading with your in-camera light meter and bracket your exposures—heavily—by at least two stops over and under the recommended setting. If you write down each setting, you can compare your notes with your photos and determine which settings are most appropriate for nighttime shooting. Recording exposures will at least give you a starting point for your next nighttime shooting session.

As with daylight photography, shutter speeds play an important role in nighttime shooting. If your scene includes moving cars, select a slow shutter speed to blur the headlights and taillights. This can be anywhere from 1/30 second to several seconds.

Standard, wide-angle, and telephoto lenses can be used to document cities after dark. For interesting photographs that burst with color and action, try shooting with a zoom lens. The technique here is to select a slow shutter speed and zoom from the longest to the shortest setting during the exposure. This technique takes some time to perfect, so experimenting with different shutter speeds and the rate at which you zoom is very important. Also, due to the long exposures, you'll need to use a tripod to steady your camera.

Special effect filters also can enhance nighttime scenes. A star filter breaks each point of light into a starburst, while a fog filter softens the harsh lights of city buildings. There is even a speed filter that creates streaks of light behind a stationary subject, creating the illusion that the subject is moving.

Here's one final tip for shooting after dark: Don't get so involved in shooting street scenes

that you forget to keep on eye on the traffic. In
fact, "wearing white at night" is a good idea for
after-dark shooters.

Taking Pictures in Museums

Taking pictures in museums requires a quiet camera, fast film (ISO 200 or 400), and perhaps a camera support. (photo #32, page 148)

At the entrance to most museums, one of the following signs is usually displayed: "No Pictures" or "No Flash Pictures." When you see the sign that says "No Pictures," you are out of luck if you want to document your day at the museum. However, if you are allowed to take pictures but cannot use a flash, you are in luck, if you are prepared for low-light level photography.

Museum objects usually are illuminated by either daylight or incandescent bulbs. For daylight pictures, I recommend fast daylight-balanced color print or slide film. A fast film will allow you to shoot with relatively high shutter speeds (to help prevent the effects of camera shake).

If you don't know the light level at the museum, it's a good idea to pack a few different film types in your camera bag. This way, you'll be prepared for different shooting situations.

For subjects illuminated by incandescent bulbs, you'll need to shoot with a tungsten-balanced film like Ektachrome 160T. When the light level is very low, this film can be pushed to ISO 320 for increased sensitivity to light.

Even when shooting with fast films, you may need to shoot at a long exposure, perhaps up to a second or two, to compensate for the relatively low light levels encountered in most museums. Long exposures require a tripod or other camera support to steady your camera and prevent camera shake. But even if you use a tripod, you can cause camera shake when you press the shutter release button. To reduce the chance of camera shake, secure your camera to the tripod, select the self-timer mode, and then release the shutter. Ten seconds or so later, the shutter will be released—smoothly.

Due to the variety of objects in most museums, you should be prepared with at least three lenses: a macro lens for close-ups of small objects in glass cases, a wide-angle lens for full-length views of statues, and a telephoto lens for subjects you can't get close to.

In museums, you need to be very quiet when taking pictures. This is not possible with most of today's automatic 35mm AF SLRs that have built-in film advance systems.

If you are very serious about taking pictures in a museum with your 35mm AF SLR, you can buy a camera "blimp" that will muffle the sound of the motor drive. A camera blimp, which sells for under $100, also can be used when photographing wildlife with sensitive ears.

Architecture

I shot this building for the cover of a local magazine on the island of Mystique. When composing the scene, I left "dead space" at the upper left-hand corner of the frame for the magazine's name. (photo #35, page 149)

Professional architecture photographers have fancy (and very expensive) cameras that help them capture the true beauty of a building. Often, a view camera, mounted atop a sturdy tripod, is used. A view camera, with its movable lens, lets the photographer capture the building in such as way as it does not look like it is falling over backward, as is often the case when a building is photographed at close range with a wide-angle lens.

An alternative to a view camera is a 35mm camera with a shift lens. A shift lens shifts like the lens on a view camera and delivers professional results. Shift lenses are available for most professional 35mm AF SLRs, like Nikon's N8008s and F4 models. In addition to shifting for special photographs, they can be used as standard wide-angle lenses.

If you can't afford a shift lens, you can still get good pictures. When shooting with a wide-angle lens, just remember that the taller the building and the more you angle your lens upward, the more the building will look like it's leaning backward or to the side. This isn't necessarily bad, especially when you are trying to add drama to a stationary subject.

To avoid the "leaning" effect, shoot with a telephoto lens from a vantage point across or down the street that lets you fill the frame with your subject. And to capture the beautiful details of a building or other structure, use a fine-grain film like Kodachrome 64.

A good time of day to photograph buildings is in the early morning or late afternoon. Photographs taken during these hours have "warm" colors, as opposed to the "cool" colors of midday.

Photographing buildings after the sun goes down gives them special beauty. For dusk scenes, when there is still some light in the sky, you can use a fast film like daylight-balanced Ektachrome 400, which is will produce a "warm" photograph. When the sky is black, you can still use Ektachrome 400 if the buildings and street are relatively bright. However, if you want an accurate color rendition of your subject, shoot with Ektachrome 160T pushed to 320.

Remember: When photographing at night, you may need a tripod to steady your camera.

Postcard Pictures

Many professional travel photographers avoid taking postcard-type photos. But postcard pictures do bring back great vacation memories.
(photo #36, page 150)

Before I left on my first travel photography assignment 1975, Lou Jones, a well-known Boston-based professional photographer and a good friend, gave me some advice. He told me to stay away from taking postcard-type shots, and go for the more creative images. "If you want to get your pictures published," he said, "you need to shoot in the early morning and late afternoon hours for dramatic lighting effects. Try different positions to see which one best complements your subject. Finally, view the scene with different lenses to see which lens is ideal for capturing the exact image you want—not too much and not too little of the surrounding scene. Study your subject, and think before you shoot."

I took my friend's advice, and returned from my jaunt with a nice portfolio of pictures, many of which were published in leading photography and travel magazines.

Over the years, as I was able to enjoy traveling at a more relaxed pace, I started to take more "grab shots," simple pictures of landmarks taken with my camera set on automatic. To my surprise, when I showed my slides to friends and family, these were among the most popular. I found that non-professionals often can relate more to simple pictures; sometimes when they view a more creative picture, perhaps with dark shadows or strong highlights, they are not as interested in the subject. It was a fascinating learning experience.

When I travel these days, I still concentrate

on getting the most creative picture of a subject. I often get up before sunrise to capture the more dramatic color of the early morning hours. I may spend an hour talking to someone, gaining his or her confidence, before I take a picture. I also study a scene in detail, making sure that all the elements in the pictures are essential, and not distracting. Most importantly, I study the lighting, making sure that shadows are not hiding an important element in my picture. Finally, I experiment with my exposure because, quite frankly, a slightly overexposed or slightly underexposed photograph may be more pleasing than the exposure I think is "perfect" at the time.

However, I also make a conscious effort to take what my wife calls "fun shots." These are simple pictures that illustrate the more personal aspect of our trip, such as a photo of my wife in front of the local tourist trap. (Sorry, Lou.) I may even stop by the local newsstand to check out the selection of postcards to get some photo ideas.

I've found that there are three benefits to taking this approach to photography—benefits that you may realize, too. First, I find that I enjoy taking pictures more; I'm more relaxed. Second, I occasionally sell a postcard-type picture to a stock agency. Third, my slide shows are a hit, not only with family and friends, but also with children I'm trying to excite about the fascinating possibilities of picture taking—and possible careers in photography.

Aerial Photography

Taking pictures from planes provides a unique view of our world. To get this shot I used a polarizing filter to reduce the glare on the water, providing a view of the hawklike sand pattern beneath the waves.
(photo #33, page 148)

Whenever I show my slides to family and friends, my aerial photographs draw much interest. These pictures provide a unique view of an exotic location—a view that captures the imagination of the viewer.

Aerial photographs are not difficult to take, if you know a few tricks of the trade. First, because a plane vibrates, it's important not to rest the lens against the window. Rather, cup your hand around the lens and make a seal between your lens and the window. This will eliminate reflections on the window that can ruin your photograph. (Naturally, the best situation is one in which there is no window. This is why professional aerial photographers rent light planes and remove the doors before they go aloft.)

To further reduce the effect of vibration, you need to shoot at a fast shutter speed, at least 1/500 second This may mean using a medium-speed film like Kodachrome 200, which can be pushed to ISO 500 and still deliver good results.

If you want to include the plane's wing in your picture, shoot with a wide-angle lens. For pictures that include only the ground below, shoot with a telephoto lens in the 85mm–150mm range. Longer telephoto lenses can be used, but may produce blurry images if your plane is bouncing around.

Zoom lenses also can be used for taking aerial pictures. However, these lenses have relatively small maximum apertures, which in turn require shooting at a slower shutter speed or using a faster film.

As in all outdoor photography, a polarizing filter is helpful in aerial photography. This filter not only will reduce glare on water and buildings, but also will cut through the atmospheric haze through which you will be shooting.

Early morning and late afternoon flights are ideal for aerial pictures with warm colors and dramatic shadows. Pictures taken around mid-day may look a bit flat, but can still convey the beauty of a "bird's-eye view" of the world below. During these hours, a 10R (red) filter will "warm up" the "cold" colors of your scene.

Finally, if your travel plans include traveling on a small plane, talk to the pilot before takeoff. Ask him if you can sit up front, which will give you an unobstructed view for your photography. Also, don't be shy about asking the pilot to bank the plane for a better picture. In most cases, the pilot will be more than happy to accommodate you.

Tropical Photo Shoot

Heat and humidity can play havoc with films and cameras. But two simple precautions, can ensure good results: Don't store your camera in an air-conditioned room, and don't leave your camera or film in the sun.

(photo #34, page 149)

A tropical vacation. What could be more fun than taking pictures in sunny, warm conditions on a white beach in the Caribbean, on the plains of Africa, or in a rainforest in South America? Fun may be how some photographers would describe these situations. Others may use the word challenging.

The first challenge on a tropical shoot is to keep your camera and film free from condensation. When you go from an air-conditioned room to the heat and humidity of the day, lenses will fog instantly, but will take a while to defog. Therefore, it's a good idea not to place yourself and your camera in this situation. If you are staying in an air-conditioned hotel, turn off the AC and open the windows about one-half hour before you are ready to leave. This will give your camera and film time to come to air temperature.

If you will be traveling by car from site to site, don't turn on the AC. Suffering at this point from the heat is better than suffering at home when looking at fogged images.

When shooting in the tropics, you also must be prepared for instant sun showers. Pack a light plastic parka in your camera bag, as well as a plastic sandwich bag for your camera. Placed in a plastic bag, your camera will also be protected from sand and salt spray when shooting at the beach and on boats.

Walking in the tropics can be strenuous,

especially when the humidity reaches 90 percent. Therefore, when shooting in these areas I like to travel as light as possible. For general picture-taking, I use the one-lens, one-film technique: 35–135mm zoom lens and Kodachrome 200. This zoom lens, which features a macro mode, can adequately handle most photographic situations—from close-ups of flowers to panoramic views of beaches to portraits of residents. The ISO 200 speed film delivers pictures without noticeable grain. And, when pushed to ISO 500, it is fast enough to shoot in the shade of a rainforest.

From personal experience, I can tell you that less is often better—especially when shooting in the tropics.

Wildlife Photography

Photographing animals in their natural habitat is challenging. It can also be rewarding, if you have the proper equipment and an understanding of your subject's habitat and habits. (photo #37, page 150)

Have you ever dreamed about going on a photographic safari to Africa, where you could take pictures of lions in their natural environment? Or how about spending a week in a tropical rainforest photographing exotic birds, monkeys, and jaguars? It's a beautiful dream, one you share with many photographers, and one that may seem out of reach. However, even if you don't have the opportunity to travel to faraway places, you can still get great environmental photos of animals right here at home.

Our national parks host a plethora of birds, mammals, and amphibians. In the Florida Everglades, for example, you'll find panthers, pelicans, alligators, turtles, and black-necked stilts. In Yellowstone National Park, moose, buffalo, and bear make their home.

To capture a wild animal on film, you need an understanding of your subject's habits. You must learn where the animal eats and how it finds food, if it is an early riser or a nocturnal predator, if it is territorial, and so on. You can find this information in nature books at your local bookstore or library. For the truly dedicated photo naturalist, Petersen's publishes the following fact-filled books: *A Field Guide to Birds*, *A Field Guide to Mammals*, and *A Field Guide to Reptiles and Amphibians*.

Next you need to prepare your photo gear. The first thing to remember is to always carry the right equipment; never carry more gear than necessary. A too-heavy load can slow you down and result in a missed shot.

A basic system for wildlife photography should consist of one or two 35mm camera bodies, a 200mm or 300mm telephoto lens for distance shots, and a 24mm or 35mm lens for pictures that include both an animal and some of the surrounding area.

Your choice of film for wildlife photography also is very important. Because you may be working in a variety of different habitats at different hours of the day, you need to be prepared for shooting in bright sunlight as well as in the shade. When shooting in daylight hours, use a slow film (ISO 25, 50, 64, or 100). When shooting in dimly lit areas or in the low-light levels of pre-dawn and dusk, you'll need to shoot with a fast film, such as Kodachrome 400 for slides, or Kodak Gold 400 for color prints. Fast films also are recommended when photographing fast-moving subjects and when using telephoto lenses or zoom lenses with apertures in the $f/4.5$ or $f/5.6$ range. Keep in mind that the faster the film, the more grain you'll get in your picture.

The proper clothing also might help you get the kind of animal photos you see in *National Geographic* magazine. Dark green or brown clothing is suitable for shooting in many outdoor situations; blending in with the surrounding area and making you less visible to your subjects. White clothing will help camouflage you in winter. If you are serious about staying hidden from view, take a trip to your local camping or hunting store. Here you'll find camouflage sportswear that will make you almost invisible, to some animals at least.

Several accessories will assist you in your

quest for beautiful wildlife photos. A tripod will help steady a camera with a long lens. A remote control unit (available for many SLRs) will help you capture a subject even if you're several hundred feet away from your camera. A 2x teleconverter will double the effective focal length of your lens for ultra-close-ups of faraway subjects. And plastic bags will protect your delicate equipment from the elements.

When you are in the field, please respect the animals. Don't feed or tease them. There's no satisfaction in taking home a prize-winning photograph when you know you may have harmed the animal in the process of making it.

Underwater Photography

I've been taking underwater pictures for four-teen years. For me, swimming beneath the waves with a camera is one of my greatest joys in life. By looking at subjects through the viewfinder, I can focus my mind on individual events—sepa-rating myself from the "big picture," which in all its beauty and splendor can be quite over-whelming.

To get good underwater pictures these days, I have an arsenal of camera equipment. I usu-ally dive with two cameras (one for wide-angle and one for macro photography) with strobes—and my wife/photo assistant dives with yet an-other system. On my dive boat or at the hotel, I have at least two back-up systems. And I bring along lots of batteries and film, a tool kit, and duct tape.

When I got started, though, I had only one Nikonos camera, one 15mm lens, and one flash. With this basic system, I got some pretty good pictures—ones I still use today in my slide shows.

If you'd like to get started with a basic sys-tem, here are ten tips that will help you get a high percentage of good pictures.

1. Think very carefully about what camera you'd like or need. If you plan to do a lot of diving, don't buy a camera that won't let you expand as your hobby does, and don't buy a system that will "break the bank" if you plan to take only one dive trip a year.

The underwater envi-ronment offers endless photo opportunities—for both wide-angle and close-up photography. (photo #s 38 & 39, page 151)

There are four basic systems to choose from:
Underwater camera housing. Designed for most AF SLRs. Most housing companies offer ports that can be used with lenses from 16mm to 90mm (macro). Some housing manufacturers even offer ports for 8mm fish-eye and zoom (usually 35–70mm) lenses.

Nikonos V. An amphibious 35mm viewfinder camera with professional lenses and accessories:
• 15mm and 20mm lenses—wide-angle lenses with good depths of field. The pro's choice for full-frame pictures of divers and reef scenes.
• 28mm lens—a good lens for fish and reef pictures.
• 35mm lens—easy-to-use for high-quality snapshots. This lens is sold with the Nikonos camera body.
• 80mm lens—used primarily for close-up photography with a close-up kit.
• Close-up kit—Includes a lens that fits over the 28mm, 35mm, and 80mm lenses and wire framers for each lens. The wider the lens in use, the larger the framer. With the 28mm lens and close-up kit, you can get a full-frame shot of a sleeping eight-inch-long parrot fish.

Nikonos RS. An amphibious 35mm autofocus SLR camera with three accessory lenses: 28mm, 20–35mm zoom, and 50mm macro.

Sea & Sea MotorMarine II. Easy-to-use point-and-shoot 35mm rangefinder camera with built-in flash unit. High-quality accessory lenses for wide-angle and close-up photography and flash units are available.

2. Read your camera instruction manual carefully. Basically, it should contain all the information you need to get good pictures.

3. Test your equipment before your dive trip. Spend a few sessions in your local swimming pool practicing wide-angle photography, and shoot a few rolls of a submerged object in your bathtub to check out macro capabilities. (I still do these at-home tests whenever I get a new piece of gear.)

You need to do these in-water tests for three reasons. First, some lenses are designed specifically for underwater photography, and out of water they produce soft images. Second, refraction causes a lens to see slightly more of a scene under water than it sees top side. So, for framing tests with close-up lenses, you need to shoot in water to determine the precise image area. Out of water, you'll get the framer in your photos. And third, it's not impossible that even a new camera can flood. If this does happen, it's better to be at home than in a far-away location. To minimize the chance of flooding, carefully grease all O-rings before each dive—and triple check all seals.

4. On site, have your film processed after your first dive. This way, you can determine what you are doing right and wrong.

5. Rather than trying to get thirty-six pictures during a dive, go for a few really great shots. Under water, there are so many variables that often you need to bracket to get one perfect picture.

6. For natural light pictures, dive shallow— above thirty feet. This is where you'll find the most color and light. When taking natural light pictures at these depths, try using Kodak's Underwater Ektachrome slide film, which is designed specifically for use under water. (This film also can be used with a strobe when filters are placed over the strobe.)

7. When shooting with a strobe, follow what famous *National Geographic* photographer David Doubilet recommends: Take the damn strobe off the camera! By positioning the strobe off camera, you can create more interesting lighting effects. In addition, you reduce the chance of getting "backscatter" (which looks like snow) in your pictures. Backscatter is caused by light from the strobe reflecting off floating particles in the water.

8. Try to fill the frame with the subject. This will eliminate lots of blue water—called dead space—in your pictures.

9. Generally, don't photograph a subject if it is further than six feet away. Because water is 800 times more dense than air, pictures taken at greater distances will look very soft. In addition, most underwater strobes are not designed for photographing subjects further than six feet away from the camera.

10. Don't get discouraged and give up after your first underwater photo session. Realistically speaking, you probably will not get lots of great shots. I certainly didn't on my first underwater shoot. Read books on underwater photography and subscribe to diving magazines. Simply put: Keep practicing and you'll get there.

Shooting on Safari

Ever since I was a kid I have dreamed about going on an African safari. Stalking wild animals — rhinos, lions, cheetahs, and elephants — and seeing first-hand their daily struggle for survival, seemed to me like the ultimate adventure. As I grew older, and developed a love for photography, a safari became even more attractive. What could be more exciting than capturing wild animals on film?

In August 1993 I headed off to South Africa's Exter Wildlife Ranch for my first foot and open-vehicle safari. Much to my surprise, the experience was very different — and much more challenging — than I had expected. Here are some of the most valuable tips I learned while on safari.

Winter or summer? If you don't like the heat, winter is the time to go on a safari. During the winter months (summer months in the United States), mornings and evenings are cool. Winter midday temperatures are tolerable, reaching to about 70 or 80 degrees Fahrenheit. One possible drawback to a winter safari is that there are relatively few leaves on the trees, so the background in your photos might not have a lot of color.

Summertime on the African plains can be scorching, with temperatures well into the 90s. During these months the green foliage will add color to your photos.

African safaris require planning, patience, and photo know-how. For full-frame animal portraits, I usually use a 300mm lens.
(photo #s 40, 41, & 42, pages 152–153)

Clothing. No matter what time of year you choose to go on safari, you need to dress appropriately. According to Robert Mortassagne, one of the leading tracker/guides and naturalists in South Africa, "The key is to wear clothing that reflects less light than the surrounding foliage. This way, it will be hard for the animals to spot you." Khaki and light green and gray clothing will help minimize your presence to the animals.

Another good piece of clothing advice is to wear layers, such as a T-shirt, long-sleeved shirt, and jacket. You'll need the jacket in the cool hours of morning, but by later morning it will be cool enough for a T-shirt.

Long pants are recommended for foot safaris. Although it's usually warm enough for shorts, long pants will protect your legs from scratches when walking through tall grass.

A hat with a wide brim also is a must for all safari photographers. Bright sunlight makes it more difficult to see animals that may be hard to spot anyway, and a hat will help shield your eyes. It also will help prevent strong light from entering the camera's viewfinder, which, on some SLR cameras, can cause an incorrect exposure reading.

Sneakers will make your hikes through the bush comfortable. However, they won't protect your toes from the sharp, two-inch-long thorns on the paths. Therefore, it's best to wear hiking boots with semi-hard soles. But before you go, break them in so you don't get blisters in the field.

Medications. Malaria is a threat in South and East Africa. Take malaria pills to minimize the possibility of contracting the disease. Because there are several strains of malaria, some of which are resistant to certain malaria medications, you'll need to consult with your physician, or the Center for Disease Control in Atlanta, Georgia, as to which medication is recommended for your destination.

Use bug spray to minimize the chances of getting a bite from a malaria-carrying mosquito or some other disease-bearing insect. For maximum protection on foot safari, you may want to do what the tracker/guides do: Spray your clothes and exposed skin with kerosene.

It's also adviseable to pack anti-diarrhea pills. In the bush, miles from camp, the last thing you want is to get hit with the runs.

Gear. When I go into the field, I take as much gear as I can carry—three 35mm Canon EOS-1 AF SLR camera bodies and eight AF lenses. However, after a two-hour walk in the bush on my first African foot safari, my two twenty-five-pound bags felt like two one-hundred-pound anvils after—and we were were still two hours from camp! By the end of the hike I was totally exhausted—and I had to ask a fellow traveler to help me with one bag. (Was this photographer/writer, member of the Explorers Club, and world traveler embarrassed? You bet!) If you're going on a foot safari, travel as light as possible.

Films. Foot and open-vehicle photo safaris usually leave camp around 6 A.M., the time of day when many diurnal animals begin their search for food. These early morning trips usually last until 10 A.M., when the animals begin to settle down and seek shelter from the hot sun. Midday, things are usually quiet in the bush, making this a good time for you to catch up on your sleep. Around 4 P.M., when it begins to cool off, the animals start to stir and the second journey into the bush begins. After dark, the safari continues in open Land Rovers. On these adventures, guides use powerful spotlights to scan the surrounding area for animals.

With such a variety of lighting conditions, different film types are essential. On sunny days, fast films such as Ektachrome 200 and 400 color slide film are sensitive enough to capture scenes at early morning and dusk. If ISO 400 slide film does not give you a fast enough shutter speed to stop action or prevent camera shake, you can push it to ISO 800. Just remember that the faster the film speed, the more grain you'll have in your pictures.

From morning to afternoon, Kodak's Elite 100 or Lumiere 100 are good all-around films for photographing the animals as well as the scenery. These medium-speed films offer superb sharpness and, in bright conditions, usually provide a fast enough shutter speed to hand-hold even a 300mm lens.

If you're photographing spot-lit animals at night with a fast ($f/2.8$) lens, ISO 400 or 800 daylight-balanced slide films allow for usable shutter speeds but not completely accurate color. For true color use tungsten-balanced Ektachrome 160 slide film pushed to ISO 320. Or use ISO 400 color print film, which usually is color-corrected in the lab.

Another option for nighttime photographs is to use daylight-balanced slide film and an on-camera flash. Most top-of-the-line flashes can illuminate subjects at forty to fifty feet.

And always bring more film than you think you'll need. I shot eighty rolls in ten days—about twenty more rolls than I had expected. Fortunately, I had packed an adequate supply of several different film types.

Lenses. You can great pictures on safari using just three basic lenses: a 300mm or 400mm, an 80–200mm zoom, and a 35–135mm zoom. The long telephoto lenses (300 or 400mm) usually let you fill the frame with an animal (the tracker/guides do get you that close!). Sometimes the 80–200mm lens will do just fine. The 35–135 zoom is good for general picture taking, snapshots, and landscape pictures.

Flash units. A flash unit is an essential accessory for a photo safari. At night, when an animal is outside of a guide's spotlight range, a flash will help you get an otherwise impossible shot. In addition, a flash can add color and detail to dawn and dusk shots of animals, if they are within relatively close shooting distance.

Camera supports. Although I packed a tripod and unipod for my photo safari, I used neither. Rather, because I had fast film and fast lenses, I was able to hand-hold my camera in most situations. When the light level was too low, I used a bean bag on the hood of the Land Rover or on a tree branch to steady my camera.

When hand-holding your camera, always select a shutter speed as fast as or faster than the focal length of the lens you're using. For example, with a 300mm lens, use a shutter speed of at least 1/300 second.

Shooting for a slide show. A safari is a truly unique adventure, and for most, a once-in-a-lifetime experience. Others may never have the chance to trek through the bush and happen upon a rhino, lion, or cheetah. A slide show of your adventure would surely be a hit with your family and friends.

When you're on safari, try shooting with a slide show in mind. Imagine that your picture will tell the entire story of your adventure, from sunrise to sunset. Shoot sequences of the life and death struggles you see, and of the more gentle interplay between animals. Your slide show will bring your experiences to life, and will educate armchair travelers about the wonders of wild animals.

Guides. Before you leave home, make sure you have an experienced guide lined up who can not only locate the animals but protect you from them as well—especially on foot safaris. Remember, you'll be walking near wild animals who may be hiding, resting, or feeding in the surround tall grass. If you startle an animal or it if feels threatened, it might leap into your path or charge.

A good guide will get you just close enough to the animals for good pictures, but not too close for comfort. In a life-threatening situation, the guides do have high-powered rifles that can stop an animal in its tracks.

Safari guides are usually excellent scanners and trackers, and will teach you to scan and track effectively. To spot animals in the wild, scan the brush from right to left. This technique slows your head/eye movement, which usually is left to right.

Tracking is a bit more difficult. First you will learn to identify and follow different hoof and paw prints under ideal conditions. Then you'll move on to systematic tracking, which is the gathering of information from signs (including hard-to-read prints) you find in the field.

Finally, you'll be briefed on speculative tracking. Here you learn to combine systematic tracking with a knowledge of animal behavior and the terrain.

It takes years to become an expert tracker. But the tracking and scanning techniques you learn will add to your safari experience. Undoubtedly you will develop a greater respect for nature and wild animals, and for the trackers who guide your way.

Part 4: Picturing Your World

Personality Portraits

On a visit to the post office a couple of years ago, I noticed a new picture of President Bush on the wall. He was smiling and well dressed; it was a professional portrait, expertly lighted and carefully composed.

Photographs of people engaged in their favorite sport or pastime capture the personality of the individual. (photo #43, page 154)

When I returned home, I saw Mr. Bush's picture in the newspaper. This time he was in his casual clothes, rod in hand, fishing from the back of a boat in Maine.

I preferred the latter photograph. It showed Mr. Bush doing something he loves, and captured a part of his personality—a love of the outdoors—to which many of us can relate.

The moral of this photographic encounter is that if you really want to get a natural-looking picture of a family member or friend, set up the picture in a natural environment, where the person is involved in his or her hobby or avocation.

Indoors. If your son plays the guitar, for example, pose him with instrument in hand. If your daughter loves a special toy, get some shots of her playing with it.

For natural-looking pictures, you'll want to use as much natural light as possible. Natural light adds a soft touch to pictures, as opposed to straight-on flash photographs that have harsh lighting and deep shadows.

There are three important elements needed for indoor natural-light portraits. First, you'll need a fast film (ISO) 400. Second, you'll need to shoot by a window. Third, you'll need a sunny day.

Fast film delivers good results when you are shooting indoors by big windows on sunny days. However, I recommend having your subject face the window, so the light is falling on his or her face. Side-lighting can add a nice effect, and back-lighting will create a silhouette. You may want to experiment to see which angle of lighting you prefer. Of course, you can always use a flash, which, when balanced with daylight, can produce very pleasing photos.

Outdoors. Personality portraits taken outdoors require planning, too. Have your subject bring his or her sports gear—golf clubs, tennis racquet, baseball glove, skiing or scuba equipment—to an appropriate setting.

As with indoor personality portraits, you want to capture some of the surrounding area in your picture. For example, you can pose a tennis player on the court, close to the net, and shoot from the opposite side of the net. For action shots, such as a golfer swinging a club or a Little League player making a grand slam, compose your picture with your subject in the center two-thirds of the frame, surrounded by the environment.

Sunny days are nice for taking outdoor portraits, but watch for harsh shadows caused by an overhead sun on your subject's face. For a softer image, with no harsh shadows, shoot on an overcast day or use a fill-in flash.

Films with ratings of ISO 100 and 200 can be used to take outdoor personality portraits. To capture the action of a golf or tennis swing, you'll need a faster film to "freeze" the action. For this I recommend using ISO 400 or even 1000 film.

One final tip on personality portraits. Talk to your subject throughout the session, and discuss the activity at hand. Silence is deadly when taking pictures of people. It makes them feel uncomfortable and self-conscious. Just a few simple comments from you will put your subject at ease, and will help you capture the true personality of your subject.

Window Light

Soft, even lighting in portraiture is easily accomplished by placing your subject near a bright window.
(photo #45, page 155)

Have your ever tried to take a natural-looking portrait of a loved one, only to be disappointed with the harsh lighting the on-camera flash or direct sunlight produced?

If so, you might want to try an often over-looked photographic technique that produces very pleasing results: posing your subject indoors by a bright window.

It sounds too simple to be true, right? But even professional photographers use this technique, for three good reasons: Window light flatters a subject, softening the skin and features; the subdued lighting does not make the subject squint; and a photographer working without a flash is much less intimidating than a "flashgun Casey."

Sunny days are recommended for indoor, natural-light portraits. When there is sufficient sunlight falling on your subject, you will be able to shoot at a high shutter speed and hand-hold your camera. On cloudy days, you will be shooting at a slower shutter speed, which may require the use of a tripod and thus restrict you and your subject.

It's also best to plan your portrait session at the time of day that provides maximum illumination at the window at which you will be shooting. For example, if you plan to shoot at a window that faces west, shoot in the late afternoon; if the window faces east, plan an early morning session.

Depending on the amount of light falling

on your subject and the effect you are trying to create, you can shoot with films that have an ISO rating of 200 or higher. As you increase the film speed, you need less illumination, but you also increase the amount of grain in your photograph. Don't be afraid of grain—sometimes it can actually enhance a portrait by softening the subject's features.

If you are very serious about getting a great portrait, do what the pros do: Take lots of pictures. Vary the position of your subject for different lighting effects. Stand between your subject and the window and take a series of pictures with your subject looking at you (front lighting), then to the left and to the right (side lighting).

Next, try another side-lighting pose. Both you and your subject stand with a shoulder near the window. Again, have your subject look out the window and then at the camera.

Here's another professional technique: Have an assistant hold a piece of white cardboard near the room-side of your subject's face. This will reflect a small amount of light back onto the subject, increasing the illumination in the shadow areas of your portrait. For increased reflected illumination, cover the cardboard with aluminum foil.

When shooting indoors—as in all photography—the background is very important. If your subject has light hair, try to compose your picture with a dark background. You might have to draw the shades or drapes to accomplish this. When photographing subjects with dark hair, a lighter background can be achieved by turning on the room lights and opening the curtains.

Although you will be using professional

techniques, you don't need professional equipment. Virtually any 35mm automatic camera will deliver good results if you fill the frame with your subject. This will help the camera's light meter determine the correct exposure.

Remember to talk to your subject, but don't use that old "Say cheese!" technique. Rather, engage your subject in a relaxed conversation, about his or her hobby or a recent trip, perhaps. This will evoke positive and natural responses, which will enhance your natural-looking portrait.

Group Photos

Every family has a "designated photographer." Throughout the years this individual is presented with many photographic challenges: working with small infants, shooting indoors in dimly lit areas, covering a wedding, taking a formal portrait of mom and dad, and so on. All these assignments require care and attention to detail. However, one of the most challenging tasks for photographers (and this goes for professionals, too) is taking group photos.

Group photos require a wide-angle lens. When choosing a lens, remember this: The larger the group and the smaller the room, the wider the lens you'll need. For example, a 35mm lens will most likely be adequate for photographing small groups in large rooms, while a 28mm lens is more appropriate for photographing large groups in small rooms. For very large groups, you may need to shoot with a 24mm lens.

One of the key elements in successful group portraits is posing the individuals so that everyone looks comfortable. With large groups, it helps to position tall people in back and short people in front. With very large groups, you may need to seat some individuals in the first row.

Next you need to make sure that everyone's face is clearly visible. This may take some fine-tuning of your subjects' positions, but it is worth the extra effort.

Before you start photographing a group, make sure that all the subjects will be evenly lighted. Outdoors, this can easily be accom-

Good group photos are the result of careful posing, even lighting, and shooting at precisely the right moment—when everyone is smiling and looking directly at the camera. (photo #44, page 154)

plished by shooting on overcast days, when harsh shadows caused by direct sun are eliminated; or by shooting with a 35mm SLR with an on-camera flash that offers automatic daylight fill-flash.

Indoors, getting an evenly lighted group can be a bit more of a challenge. If you are using an on-camera flash for direct lighting, you need to check (beforehand) the angle of flash coverage, which must be at least equal to the angle of view of the lens in use. This information is supplied with all flash units and lenses.

Some accessory flash units feature a built-in power zoom flash head that automatically zooms to the focal length of the lens in use—usually from 24mm to 85mm. This feature helps to evenly distribute the light when shooting at different focal lengths.

Direct lighting helps to produce sharp group portraits. However, for more flattering photos, you can soften the light by aiming the flash head toward the ceiling for what's called "bounce" lighting. This technique also increases the angle of flash coverage. When "bouncing" light, you need to keep in mind the following two points: One, the color of the ceiling will be reflected onto your subjects, so it's best to "bounce" the light off white ceilings only; two, "bouncing" the light reduces the effective flash distance, so you may have to work closer to your subjects.

During your photo session, you need to get and keep your subjects relaxed. Talk to them during the entire photo session. Keep them happy. Remember, everyone must look good if your pictures is to be a success.

Finally, take lots and lots of pictures. The larger the group, the more pictures you'll have to shoot to get everyone with eyes open and looking good.

Preserving Childhood Memories

Ask yourself the following questions: Do you remember how happy you were at your early birthday parties? Do you remember all the fun you had at your very first visit to the beach or local park? Do you remember the joy you felt at age three or four during the holidays? If you are like most adults, the answer is no. However, you parents may have assured you that you had a very happy childhood.

Words from loving parents are nice for children who have reached adulthood and want to know about their early development, but to use the old adage, "A picture is worth a thousand words." This is why it is so important to document all the different phases of your child's life—for your child.

You probably take dozens or maybe even hundreds of pictures of your child to show and send to family members and friends. However, it's also important for an adult to see the love and care they were given as a child by their parents, grandparents, aunts, uncles, and godparents.

In some cases, these pictures will provide a precious record of sharing a tender moment with a loved one who has passed away.

Precious memories, such a child's first bicycle ride, can be relived through the magic of photography. (photo #46, page 156)

Picturing Your Possessions

Certainly, this is not an art-quality photograph. However, when making an insurance claim, this type of photo can prove invaluable. (photo #47, page 156)

I have two sets of prints that I've never shown anyone. In fact, I hope I never have to show them to a single person. Both sets of prints are identical: They're pictures of all my worldly possessions, inside and outside my home.

I've gone through the effort of making this photographic inventory for one very important reason. In the case of a natural disaster, fire, or theft, I want my insurance company to know exactly what I had. In addition, since I carry a "replacement value" policy, I want the company to know exactly what items I want replaced, not similar products of lesser value.

Each set of prints is in a 9-by-12-inch envelope. Along with the prints is a list of my possessions, noting serial numbers when available. I keep these two envelopes in separate places, one in a fire-proof safe in my home and one in my safe deposit box at the bank. By keeping them in different places, I'm assured easy access to what may turn out to be my most valuable possession.

I've photographed everything, from my small clock radio to my rather large picnic table. When I bring home a new item, such as my new programmable telephone, I take two snapshots and put the prints in the envelopes.

My around-the-house pictures wouldn't win any awards (except those given out by my insurance company). They're uncreative snapshots, with no fancy lighting or composition.

I have been documenting my possessions for the past fifteen years. So have most of my friends. If you have not done this simple procedure, I highly recommend you do so in the near future. Plan to spend a morning or afternoon on this project. Buy a few rolls of thirty-six—exposure film, put on some music, and shoot away. Photograph each room setting, including your closets. Photograph jewelry, books, and kitchen appliances in groups. Enjoy the process, but make sure you get everything on film, including the fine details on expensive jewelry.

Virtually any camera can be used for this photo documentation project. When photographing a room, use a fast film (ISO 400), turn on all the lights, and shoot with your camera flash turned on. The room lights may give an added sense of warmth to the picture, and fill in some of the shadows caused by the flash.

Close-ups of jewelry are a bit tougher. If your camera doesn't have a macro setting or if you don't have a macro lens, you can purchase an inexpensive close-up attachment for your standard lens. After your photo documentation project, you can use your close-up lens for creative photography. It will help you get dramatic images of flowers and insects.

For amateurs as well as professional photographers, there is another advantage to going through the sometimes emotional process of documenting one's possessions. As time moves on, we all discard some of our lifestyle accessories for one reason or another. By documenting your surroundings, you'll have a time capsule of certain periods in your life. This time capsule will bring back memories not only of inanimate objects, but of family and friends who gave you meaningful gifts in years gone by.

Photography As Wall Art

Enlargements that capture the beauty of nature are ideal for decorating your home with photographic art.
(photo 48, page 157)

If you are like most picture-takers, your favorite pictures are the ones you take yourself. Your photographs represent an aspect of your personality, and they graphically illustrate how you see the world.

You probably have something else in common with fellow shutterbugs. You enjoy sharing your memories and experiences with family and friends.

But what do you do with your very best pictures? Show them once and then file them away? I hope not. Rather, why not consider making large prints and decorating your home or office with your own photographic art?

Photographic art is "in." Original prints are eye-catching conversation pieces. If several photographs are related in subject matter, such as exotic African animals, they can create a theme for a room.

To begin decorating with photographic art, you need quality enlargements. For the sharpest enlargements, you'll need to photograph with a fine grain film, such as Elite 100. Faster films (ISO 200, 400, and 1000) have more grain, and produce images that are not as crisp as those produced from slower films.

But keep in mind that grain sometimes enhances a scene. In fact, some pros use the grain in fast films to their advantage, creating dreamlike scene with a very soft quality. Even so, if the grain is the first thing someone notices in a picture, the photo is probably not worth enlarging.

Kodalux, a nationwide photofinisher, offers sixteen-by-twenty-inch poster prints that are available through most photo dealers. If you need large murals, custom mail-order labs, such as LaserColor Laboratories of West Palm Beach, Florida, make enlargements of up to six by nine feet—large enough to fill an entire wall with just one image.

Most photofinishers offer a variety of print surfaces, including glossy, non-glossy (or matte), and even a simulated canvas texture. Before you order an enlargement, however, I suggest trying to visualize how your image will look when it's printed on different types of paper. For example, if you think your picture might look good as an oil painting, you may want to go with the canvas texture. Landscapes traditionally look best on non-glossy paper, and scenes with lots of sea or sky are well suited for printing on glossy paper.

Mounting is another aspect to consider when decorating with photographic art. A fast, easy, and economical method of mounting is to ask your photo lab to mount your print on Foamcore (a type of ridged Styrofoam board), and cover the edges with black decorative tape. The result is a lightweight picture that is easy to affix to any wall.

For a more elaborate presentation, you can take your best picture down to the local framing shop and select a frame that complements your work. Wood frames enhance nature prints, while metal frames go best with pictures that have strong graphics, such as city skylines.

For clear viewing of your picture, you may want to use non-reflective glass in your frame. It's a bit more expensive than standard glass, but it does offer a clear view of pictures that are displayed in bright areas.

Finally, there is another benefit to decorating with your own photographic art in your home or office. You might even sell a print or two to a friend or your boss!

Part 5:
The Next Step

My Gear Bag

It's always a good idea to be prepared with the right accessories to meet the demands and challenges of a particular photographic situation. However, you don't want to load yourself down to a point where maneuvering around a subject is difficult.

I like to travel light. For most top-side photo assignments, I usually carry two Canon EOS-1 camera bodies and a variety of Canon lenses: a 24mm for landscapes, a 35–135mm for general picture taking, and a 80–200mm for people and animal pictures. On occasion, I'll pack a 300mm lens for close-ups of far-away subjects.

An essential accessory is my Canon EZ flash unit. I often use this accessory outdoors for daylight fill-in flash pictures.

I almost never take an outdoor picture without a polarizing filter.

My standard film choices are Kodak Elite 100 and Lumiere 100 slide film. I use Kodachrome 200 and Ektachrome 400 in low-light situations. I have all my film processed by Kodalux Film Processing Services.

Before each shooting session, I clean the front and rear elements of my lenses and dust off the inside and outside of my camera with a clean, soft cloth. I store all my equipment in a cool, dry room.

When traveling, I hand-carry all my gear, including enough film to get me through the first week of shooting—just in case my luggage is lost.

Traveling with the right accessories makes you ready for unique photo opportunities. To get this photo I needed medium-speed film, an 85mm portrait lens, and a fill-in flash unit. (photo #49, page 158)

143

Before leaving the country on a shoot, I register my gear with the U.S. Customs Office at the airport and clip the Customs form to my passport. When I return to the States, the form shows the Customs office that I did not purchase the gear abroad—and thus I don't have to pay duty.

Photo #27: *Long exposures (1/30 second to several seconds) are necessary to capture the beauty of flowing water. Because you cannot immediately see how different shutter speeds blurr the water, it's best to make several exposures at several different speeds. For this photograph I used a shutter speed of 1/8 second. Due to the relatively long exposure, I mounted the camera on a tripod.*

Photo #28 (above): *Sunsets are one of the most photogenic—and photographed—subjects. To capture the true beauty of the setting sun, you'll need to bracket your exposures. And don't always place the sun in the dead center of the scene.*

Photo #29 (opposite, top inset): *It was below zero when I took this photograph of a Russian caravan on ice-covered Lake Baikal, in south-central Siberia. Right until the moment of exposure, I kept my camera inside my warm coat—where my body heat helped to keep the camera's battery "alive." A 24mm lens provided good depth of field.*

Photo #30 (center inset): *Your typical day at the beach may not include photographing a Galapagos sea lion sunning itself. But beach photography presents lots of high-contrast situations. A dark subject on a bright, sandy background can fool your camera's meter, and thus requires a careful, close-up meter reading of the subject before you make an exposure.*

Photo #31 (bottom inset): *After sunset, you can create striking graphic images of illuminated buildings—if you have a fast film (ISO 200 or 400) and a tripod.*

Photo #32 (left): *Taking pictures in museums requires a quiet camera, fast film (ISO 200 or 400), and perhaps a camera support.*

Photo #33 (below): *Pictures taken from planes provide unique views of our world. I took this picture in Palau, Micronesia. To reduce the glare on the water I used a polarizing filter, providing a view of the hawklike sand pattern beneath the waves. Having the pilot remove the plane's door gave me a clear view of the scenery when photographing with a 24mm lens.*

Photo #34 (above): *Heat and humidity can play havoc with films and cameras. But two simple precautions can ensure good results: Don't store your camera in an air-conditioned room, and don't leave your camera or film in the sun.*

Photo #35 (left): *I shot this building for the cover of a local magazine on the island of Mystique. When composing the scene, I left "dead space" at the upper left-hand corner of the frame for the magazine's name.*

Photo #36 (left): *Many professional travel photographers avoid taking postcard-type photos. But postcard pictures, such as this popular view of St. Basil's Cathedral in Moscow, do bring back great vacation memories.*

Photo #37 (below): *Photographing animals in their natural habitat is challenging. It can also be rewarding, if you have the proper equipment and an understanding of your subject's habitat and habits.*

Photos 38 and 39: *The underwater environment offers endless photo opportunities—for both wide-angle and close-up photography. To capture this manta ray in flight, I used a 15mm Sea & Sea lens on my Nikonos V; fill light was provided by a Sea & Sea YS-200 strobe. I photographed this brittle starfish with a 60mm lens on my housed SLR; two flash units provided shadowless lighting.*

Photos 40, 41, and 42: *African safaris require planning, patience, and photo know-how. You'll need to plan your trip so that you'll be on safari at the best time of year to see animals, which usually is during the February spring migration. You'll need patience, because often you'll have to wait near watering holes for the animals to show up. And you'll need photo know-how, because the "perfect" safari photo often is gone in the blink of an eye—or the flick of a tail. For full-frame animal portraits, I usually use a 300mm lens. To record the feeling of the environment, I use a 24mm lens. My standard safari film is Kodak's Elite 100.*

Photo #43 (left): *Photographs of people engaged in their favorite sport or pastime capture the personality of the individual. When taking portrait photos, ask your subject how he or she wants to pose.*

Photo #44 (below): *Good group photos are the result of careful posing, even lighting, and shooting at precisely the right moment—when everyone is smiling and looking directly at the camera. This photo of the committee that selected the "Seven Underwater Wonders of the World" in 1989 illustrates these points. (Photo © Susan Sammon)*

Photo #45: *You can easily achieve soft, even lighting in indoor portraiture by placing your subject near a bright window. When shooting indoors, pay extra attention to the background, which can make or break a photo.*

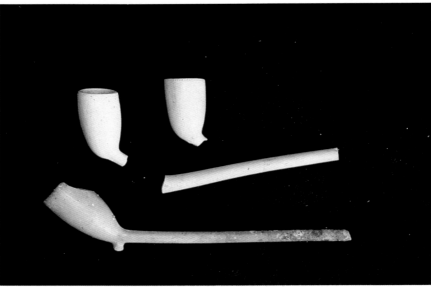

Photo #46 (top): *Precious memories, such a child's first bicycle ride, can be relived through the magic of photography. Don't skimp on film when taking photos of your children. (Photo of Rick Sammon at age five by Robert M. Sammon, Sr.)*

Photo #47: *Certainly this is not an art-quality photograph. But when making an insurance claim, this type of photo can prove invaluable.*

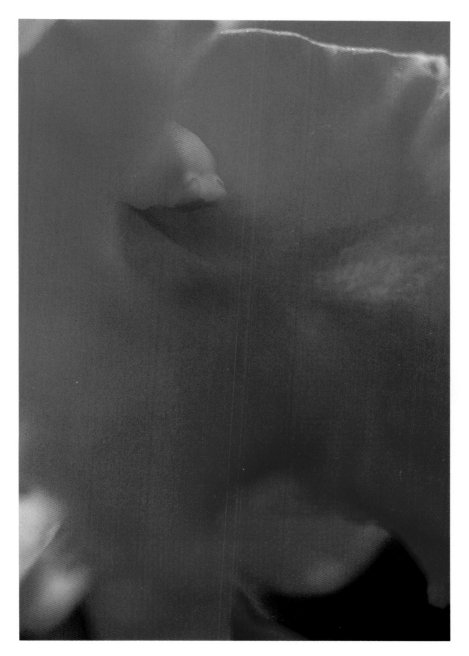

Photo #48: *Enlargements that capture the beauty of nature are ideal for decorating your home with photographic art. This ultra–close-up of a flower was taken with a 60mm macro lens on my SLR, which I mounted on a tripod.*

Photo #49 (left): *Traveling with the right accessories makes you ready for unique photo opportunities. To get this photo I used an 85mm portrait lens, a fill-in flash unit, and medium-speed film (ISO 50).*

Photo #50 (below): *This twenty-five-year-old slide, which has been published dozens of times, is still in good condition—thanks to careful handling and dark storage in an archival slide sheet.*

Photo #51 (above): *Professional travel photographers are skilled individuals with a host of talents that are necessary to capture interesting images—such as recess at this Hong Kong school.*

Photo #52 (left): *If you have sharp, well-composed images that tell a story, you may have a shot at getting your pictures published. The key to getting published is to identify potential magazines, newspapers, and book publishers that may be interested in your work.*

Exposure Data

Recording exposure data, and comparing it to your pictures, can help you determine what went wrong (or right) when going through your pictures. Make several copies of the blank Exposure Data Sheet shown here and fill it

in (as shown in my example) when testing new equipment and film. The time you spend recording this information will be well worth the effort, especially when you plan to take new gear along on a vacation.

Exposure Data	**Exposure Data**
Date: _____	Date: _____6/6/91_____
Location: _____	Location: _Moscow_____
_____	_____
Lighting conditions: _____	Lighting conditions: _sunny_
_____	_____
Time of day: _____	Time of day: _2 p.m._____
Subject: _____	Subject: _soldier_____
Camera: _____	Camera: _Canon EOS_____
Mode: _____	Mode: _Program_____
F-Stop: _____	F-Stop: _____5.6_____
Shutter speed: _____	Shutter speed: _1/250 sec._
Lens: _____	Lens: _70-210mm_____
Filter: _____	Filter: _skylight_____
Accessories: _____	Accessories: _____
_____	_____
Film type: _____	Film type: _Kodachrome 64_
Frame number: _____	Frame number: _9_____
Notes: _____	Notes: _pushed film to____
_____	_ISO 80 for better color___
_____	_saturation_____
_____	_____

Caring for Your Slides

According to the American Society of Magazine Photographers (ASMP), an original slide is valued at $1,500. This amount was arrived at due to the fact that a good stock slide can be sold several times to different book, magazine, newspaper, and newsletter publishers. Over the course of several years, an original slide may generate a total of $1,500 in sales, with individual sales ranging from $25 to $750.

With this in mind, it is very important to protect your slides. This especially holds true for travel slides, because replacing them would require a costly and time-consuming revisit to an exotic location

The key to preserving an original slide is to make a high quality duplicate transparency; you keep the original in your files while you circulate the dupe for possible sale.

Several types of dupes are available. Kodalux Processing Services offers dupes for under a dollar. These dupes are adequate for reproduction in magazines and some books, and certainly for projection in slide shows.

If you plan to see your work published in an art-quality book, you need to make a professional 70mm (about $8) or four-by-five-inch dupe (about $40) at a professional color lab. In most cases, the 70mm dupe will look almost as good as your original, and will be acceptable to the publisher for printing. For the best possible reproduction using dupes, use four-by-five-

This twenty-five-year-old slide, which has been published dozens of times, is still in good condition—thanks to careful handling and dark storage in an archival slide sheet. (photo #50, page 158)

dupes. If you're thinking about submitting original transparencies to a potential customer, be sure to keep a dupe of the original for yourself (and keep in mind that even the photos you see in *National Geographic* magazine probably have been made from dupes).

When making a pro dupe, it's a good idea to spend some time at your lab with the slide technician and discuss which format is necessary. After all, at some point it just doesn't make sense to spend all your money on dupes.

There is a way to avoid the cost of dupes: When you are shooting, take two pictures of the same subject. This way, you can circulate your "second original" and still have an original in your files.

Why do dupes get damaged by some magazine and newspaper printers? The answer is simple. The process of making color separations is a nightmare for photographers. The slide is manually cut out of the cardboard slide mount. Then it is placed on the color separating drum, and then coated with an oil to make it adhere to the drum. The drum spins while the image is scanned. Finally, the slide is removed by hand from the drum and reinserted into the slide mount. All along the way, there is the possibility of scratches and fingerprints getting on a slide. This is why dupes are invaluable.

Storing your original slides and dupes at home also is very important. For the utmost protection, it's best to store your slides in archival slide sheets (made of special plastic), as opposed to less expensive vinyl slide sheets.

Both type of slide sheets hold twenty 35mm slides and allow clear viewing of slides. But most vinyl sleeves are made with agents that can attack the emulsion of the film—ruining the slide forever. Archival sleeves, on the other hand, are chemically inert, so there is no chemical reaction with the slides.

Print File, Inc,. in Orlando, Florida, manufacturers archival sheets for slides, prints, and negatives. The company recommends that important images should be stored in a cool, dry place, preferably one that is air-conditioned. If you plan to sell your slides over a period of many years, this is good advice.

Special Skills and Talents

Professional travel photographers are skilled individuals with a host of talents that are necessary to capture interesting images.
(photo #51, page 159)

At one time or another, almost every amateur photographer dreams of becoming a professional travel photographer. Why not? They take pictures that are just as good as the images they see in newspapers and magazines. Well, they may be competent photo technicians, but working as a full-time professional travel photographer requires several special skills and talents.

If you are seriously thinking about turning travel pro, here are just a few of the attributes you'll need to survive in this highly competitive field.

Expert packer. In order to take on-location photographs, you need all your gear with you. If you are traveling by air, don't ship your cameras in your baggage. They may arrive late, or worse yet, not at all. It's best to hand-carry all your essential photo gear—no matter how heavy.

Expert traveler. If you plan to travel to faraway places, you absolutely must become an expert traveler. This means you have to double-check airline schedules; plan connecting flights; check with the Center for Disease Control in Atlanta, Georgia, to see what medication you may need to take; have your passport and visa in order; and check local communications in case of emergency.

Becoming familiar with your subject will

increase your chances of getting unique pictures. Read about the site you'll be visiting before you leave for your trip. Get a good idea of what the landscapes look like, how the local people dress, where wildlife can be found, and so on.

Film expert. Choosing which films to take along is one of the most important decisions you'll have to make. You'll also have to choose a film processor that will give you excellent results and consistent quality.

There are subtle color differences between film brands. Kodak, Fuji, Agfa, and Konica all make fine films. Some pros may swear by Kodak's Kodachrome, while others will not shoot without Fuji's Fujichrome. Again, it's up to you to decide on the film that will deliver the kind of images you prefer. The best way to determine this is to shoot test rolls of the same subject and compare results.

Always use a lead-lined pouch to protect your film from damaging X-rays at airport security stations. Also, don't buy film on the road unless it's absolutely necessary. It could be outdated and might give you poor image quality.

Still want to turn travel pro? Well, read on. In addition to adding the aforementioned titles to your imaginary resume, you also will have to develop the following skills:

Good eye. Developing an eye for photographs takes time. Again, reading about photography is a great help. Learn how the masters see light—how they capture different moods on film. Study composition; learn why the main subject does not always have to be in the center of the frame. Get a feeling for balancing several subjects in the image area; develop an eye for careful placement of background and foreground subjects.

Quick reflexes. Picture opportunities come and go in an instant. You must be ready to shoot at all times. Have your camera and flash turned on and set for automatic exposure.

Experience. Experience is a great teacher. The more you shoot, the better you will get. It's as simple as that.

Marketing Your Photos

Have you ever seen a picture in a magazine and said to yourself, "I have a shot exactly like that." Or, upon looking through a book or newspaper, said, "I could have taken that picture." If so, why not try to get some of your own photographs published, and earn some extra income as well?

If you have sharp, well-composed images that tell a story, you may have a shot at getting your pictures published. (photo #52, page 159)

The first step on the long road to getting published is to determine what publications may be interested in your pictures. The fastest way to do this is to pick up a copy of *The Photographer's Market*. This volume lists the names and addresses of virtually all the publications in the United States. More importantly, under each listing are the publication's submission guidelines and the specific types of photographs the publication needs.

Before you get your hopes up about becoming a rich and famous freelance photographer, I must mention rejection notices. These are short form letters from publishers that say, basically, "thanks, but no thanks." Receiving them is part of trying to sell your pictures. When I started freelancing, I also started a file for rejection slips. When a new one arrived, I added it to my collection. Some were humorous, others were curt. But more on dealing with rejection later.

After you pick up *The Photographer's Market*, spend some time investigating all the different possibilities for your pictures. Keep in mind that one picture could be used to illustrate several different articles. For example, if you are going to Mexico, a picture of the Mayan ruins could be used to illustrate stories on traveling to Mexico, Mayan architecture, Mexico on twenty-five dollars a day, Central American tours, and educational adventures for those over fifty. These are just a few ideas. You could probably come up with several more.

When you send your pictures to a magazine, keep in mind that editors receive hundreds of submissions a year. You'll have lots of competition, so your material must stand out. You need to send high-quality duplicate slides, a neatly typed letter, and a stamped, self-addressed envelope for the return of your slides. Never send your original slides—they could get lost in the shuffle.

You also need another key ingredient: patience. Most publications take four to six weeks to respond to photographers. If an editor is interested in your work, you'll get a call or letter. If not, your pictures probably will be returned.

The final factor in getting published is timing. Others may call it luck. Your pictures must arrive just at the right moment—when the publication is planning an article that needs illustrations. To increase your luck, therefore, it's important to work hard to keep your pictures in circulation. Don't get discouraged by rejection letters. After all, perhaps the editor loved your pictures, but just ran a similar set of photos six months ago. Or maybe he or she already has an article on your subject matter planned for sometime next year.

You may want to keep the following adage in mind while you're licking stamps and putting your slides in an envelope late on a Sunday night in the hopes of getting your pictures published: The harder you work, the luckier you'll be.

Glossary

If you are new to the exciting world of 35mm photography, the following glossary will help you become familiar with some of the technical terms—in *nontechnical* talk.

AF (autofocus) sensor
A device in a 35mm SLR autofocus camera that tells the lens where to focus. Usually, the more sophisticated the camera, the more AF sensors it has. With additional sensors, arranged both vertically and horizontally, the camera can focus on a wide variety of subjects at different distances.

Aperture
The opening in the lens that regulates the amount of light that reaches the film. At the widest aperture (lowest f-stop number), the maximum amount of light reaches the film. At the smallest aperture (highest f-stop number), the least amount of light reaches the film. As the f-stop number increases (aperture decreases), depth of field increases (on all lenses).

Aperture Priority mode
Exposure mode in which you select the aperture and the camera automatically selects the shutter speed for correct exposure. Also called *aperture-preferred mode*.

Archival slide sheets
Chemically inert plastic slide holders designed to offer maximum protection for color slides.

(Less expensive slide sheets can create a chemical reaction on the film and ruin your slides if stored for a long period of time.)

ASMP (American Society of Magazine Photographers)
An organization for professional photographers which develops business guidelines for its members.

Backlighting
Strong light from behind a subject that can create either a silhouette or an underexposed picture. Some cameras have a backlight compensation button, which automatically adjusts for this by increasing the exposure by about 1½ stops.

Blimp
A foam device that wraps around a camera to reduce motor drive and autowinder noise.

Bracketing
The technique of taking additional exposures of the same shot, under and over the recommended exposure settings—with the goal being a perfect exposure.

Camera shake
Caused by selecting a shutter speed that is too slow for hand-held picture taking, resulting a blurred picture.

Close-up lenses
Inexpensive screw-on lenses that offer close-up possibilities for normal lenses (35mm to 55mm focal lengths).

Color shift
An unnatural shift in color that sometimes occurs during extremely long exposures (longer than one second).

Data back
A device with a variety of functions, including the imprinting of time and date on film. More sophisticated data backs also can control exposures and perform time-lapse functions.

Depth of field
The area that is in focus behind and in front of a subject. Sometimes called depth of focus. Depth of field is controlled by the size of the aperture, the focal length of the lens, and the distance between camera and subject.
See also Aperture.

DX coding
DX coding marks (black and silver bars that appear on most 35mm film cassettes) that automatically tell a camera with DX coding capability certain information about the film, including the ISO number, film type, and number of exposures on the roll.

Exposure modes
See particular exposure modes.

Exposure latitude
The measure of a film's forgiveness for over- and underexposed pictures. Slide films have a *narrow* exposure latitude, so your exposure must be as close to perfect as possible. Print films have a much wider exposure latitude, so you can take an over- or underexposed picture and still get a beautiful print.

Fast film
See High-speed film

Fill-in flash
Usually, the outdoor photography technique of using an on-camera or in-camera flash to softly fill in shadows on a subject's face. Good fill-in flash pictures don't have the harsh shadows or highlights of traditional flash pictures.

Film speed
The measure of a film's relative sensitivity to light. "Fast films" (or "high-speed films") are very sensitive to light. "Slow films" are less sensitive to light. The speed of a film is represented by its ISO number.
See also High-speed film; ISO number; Slow film

Filters
See specific types of filters.

Fish-eye lens
Produces a circular image on the rectangular frame. Has a field of view of 180 degrees and offers maximum depth of field.

Fixed-lens camera
A camera that has its shutter in the lens (unlike a single-lens reflex [SLR] camera, which has a focal plane shutter). Also called lens-shutter camera or point-and-shoot camera. With a fixed-lens camera, you view the scene through a framefinder rather than directly through the lens; thus, the resulting photo may not always capture exactly what you saw.

Focal length

The length of the lens, usually measured from the center of the lens to the film plane. For example, the focal length of a 100mm lens is 100mm.

Focal plane shutter

A shutter situated directly in front of the film.

Focus lock

A feature found on most 35mm AF SLRs that lets you lock in the focus of an off-center subject and then recompose the scene.

F-stop

The various settings on a camera's aperture ring; these settings control the size of the aperture opening. The *f*-stop, or *f*-number, represents the relationship of the size of the aperture opening to the focal length of the lens. For example, an *f*-stop of *f*/16 on a 50mm lens means that the diameter of the aperture opening is 1/16 of the lens's focal length, or 3.125 mm.
See also Aperture.

Graduated filter

A screw-on filter usually used to darken the top portion of a scene so the top and bottom of the photo are of equal brightness.

Gray card

A handy accessory that provides accurate in-camera meter readings in tricky lighting situations, such as beach and snow scenes. Because exposure meters are based on 18 percent gray as the average for correct exposure, a gray card is printed in solid, 18 percent gray. The card is placed in the same light as the subject, and a meter reading is taken from the card.

Haze/skylight filter

A screw-on filter that reduces atmospheric haze in a picture, increasing the clarity of the image.

High-contrast film

Black and white film that produces only pure black and pure white, with no shades of gray. Usually used for special effects.

High-speed film

Film that is very sensitive to light; thus, it allows you to shoot at high shutter speeds to "freeze" action. Films with an ISO rating of 400–1000 are called high-speed, or fast films.

ISO number

The film speed number. For example, Kodak Elite 100 has an ISO number of 100. (Previously, *ASA number*.)
See also Film speed; High-speed film; Low-speed film

Lenses

See particular types of lenses.

Lens shade

A hood that screws into a lens's filter threads; used to prevent stray light from falling on the lens and ruining a picture.

Lens-shutter camera

See Fixed-lens camera.

Low-speed film

Film that is not very sensitive to light. Low-speed films require slow shutter speeds; thus, when shooting with low-speed film, you may have to use a camera support to prevent cam era shake. Films with an ISO rating of 50 or less are called low-speed, or slow films.

Macro lens
A close-up lens, usually with a focal length from 50mm to 100mm. Lets you get life-size reproductions of small subjects.

Manual mode
An exposure mode in which you select both the aperture and shutter speed manually, to fine-tune your exposure.

Monopod
A handy, one-legged device used to steady a camera. Designed for sports photographers who need to move around a lot.

Motor drive
A motor inside the camera that advances and rewinds the film automatically.

Polarizing filter
A screw-on filter used to reduce glare on water and glass and darken white clouds against a blue sky. Also can reduce atmospheric haze in a photo. Does not work when shooting directly into or away from the sun.

Program mode
Exposure mode in which the camera automatically selects both the aperture and shutter speed.

Remote control unit
A trigger-release device that allows you to trip the shutter from a distance.

Single-lens-reflex (SLR) camera
A camera that allows you to view the scene exactly as the camera sees it: through the lens at the front of the camera. SLRs offer a variety of interchangeable lenses and accessories.

Shift lens
A wide-angle lens used for architectural photography that shifts up and down to reduce or eliminate the effect of a building "falling" backwards.

Shutter Priority mode
An exposure mode in which you select the shutter speed and the camera automatically selects the aperture. Also called *shutter-speed-preferred mode*.

Shutter speed
The length of time the camera's shutter stays open when you take a picture. The shutter speed numbers represents fractions of a second; for example, with a shutter speed setting of 500, the shutter will remain open for 1/500 second when released.

Slow film
See Low-speed film

Spot meter
A meter, either in-camera or hand-held, that reads only a spot in the frame. A spot meter is useful for getting the proper exposure of distant light subjects positioned against dark backgrounds or dark subjects on light backgrounds.

Standard lens
The lens that is sold with a new 35mm SLR; usually a 50mm lens.

Teleconverter
An inexpensive accessory that turns a telephoto lens into a super-telephoto lens by multiplying the telephoto lens's focal length (usually by two or three times). A teleconverter fits between the lens and the camera body. Results are good with good quality teleconverters, but they don't match images taken with fixed-focal length tele-photo lenses.

Telephoto lens
A lens with a longer focal length than a normal lens; thus it brings distant subjects closer. Great for portrait and widlife photography.

Wide-angle lens
A lens with a shorter focal length than a nor-mal lens; thus it takes in a wide view. Well suited for landscape photography and for pho-tographing large groups in small rooms.

Zoom lens
A lens with variable focal length; thus it offers several lenses in one. For example, a 35mm-105mm zoom offers the shooting flexibility of a 35mm semi-wide-angle lens, 50mm lens stan-dard lens, 80mm short telephoto lens, and 105mm medium telephoto lens.

Readings

For those readers who would like more detailed information on photography—the creative aspects as well as the business angle—following is a list of suggested readings. You can order these books from your local bookstore or from the publisher.

The Art of Outdoor Photography
by Boyd Norton
Published by Voyageur Press
123 North Second Street
Stillwater, MN 55082
800-888-9653

Boyd Norton's PhotoJournal
by Boyd Norton
Published by Voyageur Press
123 North Second Street
Stillwater, MN 55082
800-888-9653

Literary Agents & Art/Photo Reps
Edited by Robin Gee
Published by Writer's Digest Books
1507 Dana Avenue
Cincinnati, OH 45207
800-289-0963

Professional Photographer's Survival Guide
by Charles Rotkin
Published by Writer's Digest Books
1507 Dana Avenue
Cincinnati, OH 45207
800-289-0963

Photo Gallery Workshop Handbook
By Jeff Cason
Published by Images Press, Inc.
7 East 17th Street
New York, NY 10003
212-675-3707

Photographer's Business and Legal Handbook
By Leonard D. DuBoff
Published by Images Press, Inc.
7 East 17th Street
New York, NY 10003
212-675-3707

Photographer's Market
Edited by Sam Marshall
Published by Writer's Digest Books
1507 Dana Avenue
Cincinnati, OH 45207
800-289-0963

Resources

Need more detailed information on accessories and services? Drop a note to the companies listed here and ask for a free brochure.

Accessory AF SLR Lenses

Tamron Industries
99 Seaview Boulevard
Port Washington, NY 11050
(516) 484-8880

Sigma Corporation
15 Fleetwood Court
Ronkonkoma, NY 11779
(516) 585-1144

Vivitar
9350 De Soto Avenue
Chatsworth, CA 91311
(818) 700-2890

Art Quality Enlargements

LaserColor Laboratories
Fairfield Drive
West Palm Beach, FL 33407
(407) 848-2000

Films

Eastman Kodak Company
343 State St.
Rochester, NY 14650
(800) 242-2424

Fuji Film
555 Taxter Drive
Elmsford, NY 10523
(800) 526-9030

Konica USA
40 Sylvan Avenue
Englewood Cliffs, NJ 07632
(800) 341-0302

Ilford Photo (black and white only)
70 W. Century Road
Paramus, NJ 07653
(201) 265-6000

Film Processing

Kodalux Processing Services
3000 Croasdaile Drive
Durham, NC 27705

Filters

Cokin Creative Filters
Minolta Corporation
101 Williams Drive
Ramsey, NJ 07446

Tiffen Manufacturing
90 Oser Avenue
Hauppauge, NY 11788
(800) 645-2522

Slide Sleeves

Print File, Inc.
P.O. Box 607638
Orlando, FL 32860

35mm AF SLRs

Canon
One Canon Plaza
Lake Success, NY 11042

Minolta Corporation
101 Williams Drive
Ramsey, NJ 07446

Leica Camera, Inc.
156 Ludlow Avenue
Northvale, NJ 07647

Nikon, Inc.
1300 Walt Whitman Road
Melville, NY 11747

Olympus America
145 Crossways Park
Woodbury, NY 11797

Pentax
35 Inverse Drive East
Englewood, CO 80112

Index

About the Author

Photo © by Susan Sammon

Rick Sammon—photographer, writer, lecturer, and international explorer—writes "Camera Angles," a weekly column for the Associated Press Special Features Service. The how-to column is circulated to approximately one thousand newspapers each week. When he's not taking pictures and writing, Rick gives photo seminars and lectures on photography.

Camera Angles is Rick's tenth book. In 1992 his conservation-oriented book *Seven Underwater Wonders of the World* was an international success. In 1993 he and his wife Susan developed two 3-D books exclusively for The Nature Company: *Under the Sea in 3-D* and *Creepy Crawlies in 3-D*.

Rick also has been published extensively in *Outdoor Photographer*, *New York Times*, *Nikon World*, *Explorers Journal*, Rodale's *Scuba Diving*, and *Popular Photography*.

Before going freelance, Rick was the editor of *Studio Photography* and *Today's Film-maker*. He also served for ten years as Vice President, Group Supervisor at Bozell Inc., one of the world's largest advertising and public relations firms. While at Bozell, Rick and fellow photographer Charlie Bray developed the LaserScape Project, a 9-foot-high by 150-foot circular panoramic mural of the Grand Canyon. To date, this is the world's largest panoramic photo mural.

Rick and Susan are directors of CEDAM International, the marine exploration organization dedicated to Conservation, Education, Diving, Archeology, and Museums. With CEDAM, the Sammons have led expeditions to many different parts of the globe. Rick and Susan also operate Sea Stock, a stock photo agency.

Rick, Susan, and their son, Marco, live in Croton-on-Hudson, New York, where they also produce the newsletter for the Croton Community Nursery School.

Camera Adventures® with AP Photographer Rick Sammon

Join Associated Press photographer Rick Sammon for in-the-field photo workshops and tours to the American Southwest, Galapagos Islands, Fiji, Costa Rica, and Africa. Scuba diving tours are also available. When writing, please specify tour destination(s).

Rick Sammon's Camera Adventures
One Fox Road
Croton-on-Hudson, NY 10520 USA